Assessing
Deeper Learning

Assessing Deeper Learning

Developing, Implementing, and Scoring Performance Tasks

Douglas G. Wren
with
Christopher R. Gareis

ROWMAN & LITTLEFIELD
Lanham • Boulder • New York • London

Published by Rowman & Littlefield
An imprint of The Rowman & Littlefield Publishing Group, Inc.
4501 Forbes Boulevard, Suite 200, Lanham, Maryland 20706
www.rowman.com

6 Tinworth Street, London SE11 5AL, United Kingdom

Copyright © 2019 by Douglas G. Wren and Christopher R. Gareis

All rights reserved. No part of this book may be reproduced in any form or by any electronic or mechanical means, including information storage and retrieval systems, without written permission from the publisher, except by a reviewer who may quote passages in a review.

British Library Cataloguing in Publication Information Available

Library of Congress Cataloging-in-Publication Data Available

ISBN: 978-1-4758-4577-8 (cloth)
ISBN: 978-1-4758-4578-5 (pbk.)
ISBN: 978-1-4758-4579-2 (electronic)

Contents

Foreword — vii
Eva L. Baker

Preface — xi

Acknowledgments — xv

Introduction — xix

1 Teaching and Assessing for Deeper Learning — 1
   Chris Gareis

2 Looking Back at Performance Assessment — 19

3 Performance Assessment versus Performance Tasks — 29

4 Embarking upon the Journey — 35

5 Ruminating on Rubrics — 45

6 Developing Performance Tasks — 57

7 Scoring Performance Tasks — 75

8 Using Performance Task Results — 89

9 Leveraging Performance Assessment in the Classroom — 101
   Chris Gareis

10 Purposeful Innovation — 117
   Chris Gareis

Appendix A	133
Appendix B	143
About the Authors	155

Foreword

Performance assessment is central to the thesis of this book, not surprisingly titled *Assessing Deeper Learning: Developing, Implementing, and Scoring Performance Tasks*. As a general strategy, it represents a commitment to provide integrated tasks to develop and determine learners' levels of expertise. A performance task may show the respondent's ability to infer important requirements, involve problem identification or search tactics, their competency in selecting central rather than peripheral elements to emphasize, and measure the process by which the outcome is reached, including mistakes and inappropriate paths.

Except in procedural learning, where the respondent is required to duplicate a particular sequence of steps in a predestined order, most performance assessments include some level of transfer or generalization. The assessment should emphasize the use of one or more principles in a new setting, the application of a schema to new content and task expectations, or a unique combination of skills not previously subject to direct instruction. Most of these aspects of performance assessment are linked to improving the quality, realism, and utility of instruction for students. All should support higher levels of student motivation.

But the desired instructional framework is by no means straightforward. It does not often depend upon the "see this, do this" model that might be found in training medical students in basic procedures. Instead, the instructional facets required to ensure serious performance assessment competency include many subtle components, depend dramatically on type and fluency of domain knowledge, and require sophisticated understanding by teachers or instructional designers.

Some of the pervasive flaws of performance assessment are identified or alluded to in this volume. Its use as a strong measurement is often limited by the "one-at-a-time" development, characterized by the search for a provocative question, but it is rarely linked to a family or domain of exchangeable performance assessments. This "one-item" development of assessments led earlier measurement experts to posit the need for many particular examples to assess a general ability.

Yet, more recent designs have addressed performance assessment in a modular way, where particular definitions and examples of cognitive requirements, such as problem solving or explanation, are given and then implemented in common or different content domains. Intentionally, we pursue the generation of a common type of performance assessments and greatly reduce the number required to estimate the level of a performance domain or ability.

Other persistent performance assessment challenges include the development of adequate and valid scoring rubrics, as many may be generated in a fairly arbitrary manner. As a contrast, rubrics not only require reliable scoring, either by individuals or computer, but also validity evidence. They may be validated, for instance, by their relationship to expert (or at least competent) performance by those thought to exhibit the desired level of learning.

For performance assessment to lead to a transformation of teaching and learning, then quality measurement must be documented. Teachers' use of performance assessment is a necessary but not sufficient condition for reform, as the criteria teachers use to judge student work will need to approximate features of any external rubrics. Sadly, not much systematic work is undertaken in this area. Related to this issue is the role of collaboration in performance assessment. Early research examined individual and group or team performance, but there remains contention about the best methods to "count" contributions.

Beyond measurement, there are both challenges and opportunities on the horizon, many of which have been noted in this excellent volume. They include understanding the subtasks required—including domain knowledge—that may need to be explicitly considered in teaching and in the judgment of student processes or products. Another essential focus is how to develop experiences that will lead to equitable and quality performance across subgroups varying by socioeconomic level, gender, and so on.

There are also a wide range of performances that currently comprise the performance assessment repertoire, including those that simulate either in reality or virtually, complex tasks; games; and composite tasks that include doing, solving, and writing. Analytics of learning processes may point the way to indicate how these components could be valued and lead to a stronger set of models for use in classroom and external assessments.

Giving the reader an opportunity to understand the uses of performance assessment set within an educational reform framework is a particular strength of this work. Prolific and clear examples help the reader understand what the method is all about. We need serious and thoughtful reform in education, particularly in an era where other countries may understand and invest in the importance of integrated skill development. Thankfully, this book provides us with crystalline guidance.

Eva L. Baker
Distinguished Research Professor of Education
Director, Center for Research on Evaluation,
Standards, and Student Testing
University of California, Los Angeles

Preface

My first teaching job was teaching first grade. I was excited to be working at a school located in my old neighborhood; the high school I attended was about a mile away. While giving back to the community was a great feeling, like many first-year teachers, most of the time I felt overwhelmed and unsure of myself. Because of the stress—something that can occur at any time during a teacher's career—I wasn't really enjoying my chosen vocation.

One afternoon while conducting a lesson via direct instruction, I had an epiphany that changed everything. I stopped talking momentarily and scanned the classroom. Nary was a first grader in my class looking at me, and it appeared that no one was listening either. At that moment, I realized my teaching methods were identical to the methods my teachers employed to teach me decades earlier.

What had I been thinking? Years of prior experience working with youth-serving agencies taught me that each new generation of children is different from the previous generation. Lecturing and teacher-directed instruction may have been effective with my contemporaries, but they didn't fly with my class. From then on, I used mainly student-centered lessons and tried novel activities and ideas—some original and others borrowed. My students were engaged in their learning and they were having fun. Teaching became less stressful and more fun for me as well.

The following spring, something else happened that changed the way I thought and taught. Per district mandate, every elementary class from first through fifth grade took the Iowa Test of Basic Skills (ITBS), a standardized multiple-choice test. What I found out from giving the ITBS to my students for the first time was that (1) many six- and seven-year-olds do not possess the fine motor skills to properly fill in small bubbles with a pencil, (2) most first graders do not have the attention span to fully focus on a test that takes an hour or two, and (3) some students are extremely anxious about taking standardized tests.

Despite my reservations about giving standardized tests to young students, I dutifully prepared my classes for the ITBS for the duration of my tenure as a primary teacher. My students practiced the art of bubbling on classroom assessments. I talked with them about why they were taking the test, dispelling myths ("This is not a pass-fail test, and you *will* get promoted to the next grade") and trying to motivate them ("You should do your best on the test. Did I mention you get Jolly Ranchers and extra recess after it's over?"). From conversations with other teachers, I learned that test fatigue and test anxiety were prevalent among older students, not to mention the teachers themselves.

There were parallels between the type of testing that predominated in my school and the type of teaching I had mostly abandoned during my rookie year. Rote instruction served the purpose of preparing students for multiple-choice tests at the classroom, district, and state levels, but I was more interested in teaching and testing that required students to use higher-order thinking skills. It was no coincidence that assessment became the main focus of my studies when I returned to graduate school at the beginning of my fourth year of teaching.

Although my educational measurement and assessment courses taught me best practices for constructing different types of tests—as well as methods to maximize reliability and validity—one question plagued me: How can educators make assessment more relevant and engaging for students? To this end, I revised existing tests and created thought-provoking tests for my students. Some of them were multiple choice.

The opportunity to develop truly innovative assessments for districtwide administration came midway through my career. When Virginia Beach City Public Schools needed performance tasks to measure the critical-thinking, problem-solving, and written communication skills of elementary and middle school students across the district, I was one of two people assigned to lead the project. This book contains a comprehensive account of the project, or journey, as I like to call it.

For years, Susan Brookhart, Linda Darling-Hammond, Jay McTighe, Chris Gareis, and other experts have extolled the benefits of performance assessment. Performance-based assessments and performance tasks are currently the rage in K–12 assessment—countless resources are available. A Google search for "performance assessment" yielded over 5.8 million results. Unfortunately, not all of the vendors, organizations, and teacher websites with performance assessment resources communicate to prospective users that performance tasks can be messy.

The usual suspects of performance tasks are time, cost, and objectivity. Good performance tasks take time to develop, administer, and score. Large-scale performance task programs can be expensive. Performance tasks involve the use of rubrics, which do not always facilitate consistent or coherent scoring. It's essentially a cascade effect: if the scoring process is not objective, the scores will not be reliable, and if the scores are not reliable, they will not be valid for their intended purposes. These are a few potential pitfalls of performance tasks.

This book was written for educators, policy makers, and others interested in learning more about developing, implementing, and scoring performance tasks. The chapters written by my esteemed colleague, Chris Gareis, serve as bookends to my chapters, which trace the journey of Virginia Beach's districtwide performance task program. Our book is a call for educators, policy makers, and other stakeholders to commence or continue the important work of assessing students' deeper learning through the use of performance tasks. For those of you who plan to set out on a similar journey, I applaud your efforts and wish you bon voyage.

Acknowledgments

Going into teaching was the smartest thing I ever did. I would like to express my most sincere appreciation to my former students and the friends I made at Evansdale Elementary School and Kittredge Magnet School in DeKalb County, Georgia. You all helped me become a better teacher and person.

Pursuing a doctorate was another good move. I had many outstanding instructors at the University of Georgia; foremost among them were Jeri Benson, Beverly Payne, and David Payne. I am indebted to these professors for the knowledge and encouragement they imparted upon me.

Jared Cotton and Chris Fischer also deserve recognition and my gratitude. Dr. Cotton hired me to work at Virginia Beach City Public Schools, and the journey described in this book would not have happened without him. Dr. Fischer was the other half of "we" during the initial stages of the journey.

I'm indebted to a few other people whose assistance made the book possible. First, I want to thank my friend and colleague Chris Gareis for sharing his expertise in the chapters he contributed. In addition, much appreciation goes out to Babette Brinkley and Sarah Hylton for providing helpful suggestions on earlier drafts of the manuscript, as well as to my friend Stephen Court for his advice, manuscript feedback, and statistical analyses.

Finally, I am deeply grateful to my family for their love and support during the many months I spent writing. Pardon the cliché, but my children are truly the light of my life. My daughter, Naomi, is an accomplished and witty scholar, and my son, Everett, is a compassionate and dedicated US Marine. My wife, Heather, is the best teacher I ever worked with—she continues to inspire countless students and educators, including me.

—Doug Wren

I met Doug Wren in October 2015 during the annual conference of the Consortium for Research on Educational Assessment and Teaching Effectiveness (CREATE), which was held in Charleston, South Carolina, that year. While I don't know what his first impression was of me, I immediately took a liking to him. His presentation on the development of large-scale, integrated performance assessments was firmly grounded in research, illustrated by real-life practice, and delivered with a unique balance of clarity and humor that I have come to expect of Doug.

Following Doug's CREATE presentation, I made a point of finding time to meet and talk with him. I wanted to know more about his work, and I wanted to learn from this very intelligent man whose commitment to public education is worn on his sleeve. As fate would have it, our nascent collegial relationship quickly morphed into friendship as we discovered that we had grown up mere miles from each other in the suburbs of Atlanta, Georgia, attended rival public schools in DeKalb County, and shared a love of the Atlanta Chiefs professional soccer team of the 1960s and 1970s.

So, when Doug asked me to partner with him on this book, I did not hesitate. Like any great teacher, Doug has led this project with a love of the topic, a penchant for organization and detail, a purposeful and wholesome diligence, a sincere and engaging style, and a genuine respect and admiration for those whom we want to serve—here, the teachers and educational leaders for whom we have written this book. I am a better thinker, writer, and teacher for my collaboration with Doug.

Of course, writing a book requires an extraordinary commitment of thought, emotion, and labor over an extended period of time. With that in mind, I would also like to acknowledge and thank a number of other individuals who have been particularly important to me during the span of this project:

- Innumerable teachers and educational leaders across the Commonwealth of Virginia for your commitment to public education and your spirit of innovation and collaboration, especially Steve Geyer, Amy Griffin, Laurie McCullough, and Autumn Nabors;
- Sarah Hylton for your keen eye and your commitment to the power of formative feedback;
- Richard Whitcomb, Chris Milner, Tommy Hughes, and Ted Cashin for a friendship good enough to last a lifetime . . . and always there when I need it
- Lisa Gareis Korslund, Peter Gareis, and Sarah Gareis Wilson for a bond that is as strong as our roles are unique;
- Mia, my constant (writing) companion;

- Hance Gareis, Isabelle Gareis, and Anne Ryan Gareis for who you are, who you are becoming, and who you help me to be; and
- Molly Gareis for a love that is (and has been for a quarter century and counting) *true* in every sense of the word.

—Chris Gareis

Introduction

Raise your hand if you've ever seen or heard this statement: "We are currently preparing students for jobs that don't yet exist . . . using technologies that haven't yet been invented . . . in order to solve problems we don't even know are problems yet."[1] A lot of people assume it is a fairly recent revelation; however, a similar statement appeared in an article published about sixty years ago in *The School Review*: "Our young people will fill many jobs that do not now exist."[2]

Educational thinkers and leaders have long recognized the need for teaching and learning to evolve, but even in the face of a rapidly changing world, education typically lags behind other professions in its ability to self-transform. While policy makers and administrators across the nation aspire to education's higher purposes, rote instruction and extensive multiple-choice testing continue to flourish in schools under their purview. Institutionalized philosophies and practices are difficult to dislodge.

When asked how teaching has changed over the years, educators frequently mention, and often praise, the technologies that have been implemented in their schools or districts. In contrast, when asked about changes that stemmed from the No Child Left Behind Act of 2001 (NCLB), veteran educators are likely to allude to its negative consequences.[3]

The goals of NCLB were admirable, but the unintended effects—increased high-stakes testing and teaching methods that cater to multiple-choice tests—led to what some have called the dumbing down of state standards and tests; teacher preparation programs; and, sadly, students.[4] The Every Student Succeeds Act (ESSA), which took effect at the beginning of the 2017–2018 school year, retained almost all of NCLB's testing obligations.

State-mandated, standardized tests have a definitive role in education. They fulfill federal accountability requirements and provide opportunities for stakeholders to identify the relative level at which students have mastered predetermined skills and content. On the other hand, the results of these tests are mere snapshots of students at a single point in time, and they offer little of value to the teaching and learning process. When the focus of a district, a school, or a teacher is on test scores, the purpose of education becomes distorted.

Discussions and debates about the true purpose of education have gone on for centuries. Some contemporary discussants and debaters agree that teaching higher-order thinking skills—often referred to nowadays as deeper learning[5]—is the primary purpose of education. Content knowledge and basic skills are vital, but students should also be taught "to think intensively and critically," as Martin Luther King Jr. argued over seventy years ago.[6] Teaching deeper learning serves two other commonly mentioned purposes of education: preparing the workforce and producing good citizens.

It is not enough to teach deeper learning; educators need to know whether their students have acquired these requisite skills. Measuring higher-order thinking requires higher-order assessments, including performance tasks that allow students to demonstrate deeper learning. Since 2010, the William and Flora Hewlett Foundation has funded efforts to deliver and assess deeper learning. One approach supported by this funding involves helping K–12 teachers implement classroom-based performance assessments.[7] Additionally, ESSA recommends "up-to-date measures that assess higher-order thinking skills and understanding, which may include measures . . . delivered in the form of portfolios, projects, or extended performance tasks."[8]

Before the Hewlett Foundation defined deeper learning and ESSA was enacted, a large school district in Virginia adopted a strategic plan that emphasized specific skills deemed essential for students to succeed in the twenty-first century. The plan called for teaching and assessing the skills, though it appeared several skills would be hard to measure. Determined to take on the challenge, the district embarked on a journey to develop, implement, and score performance tasks for assessing students' critical-thinking, problem-solving, and communication skills.

This book presents a full account of the journey, a multiyear odyssey in which many lessons were learned and various obstacles were overcome. *Assessing Deeper Learning: Developing, Implementing, and Scoring Performance Tasks* is for educators at all levels—classroom teachers to superintendents—as well as for school board members, legislators, and other people with an interest in performance assessment. It is the story of a series of performance tasks, administered annually to thousands of students, that were designed to measure deeper learning.

REVIEW OF CHAPTERS

In chapter 1, "Teaching and Assessing for Deeper Learning," Chris Gareis introduces the concept of deeper learning and describes the Hewlett Foundation's features of deeper learning. Chris delves into current understandings of teaching, learning, and assessing, and explains how deeper learning relates to the development of educational programs for today's students. Toward the end of the chapter, he makes a case for a meaningful and coherent approach to assessment, one that utilizes authentic performance tasks within a balanced assessment system.

While chapter 1 alludes to the previous century's standards-based movement and the current century's high-stakes testing movement, chapter 2 provides a more in-depth look at events spanning the past four decades that got us to where we are now. The chapter tracks the history of large-scale accountability testing, with a focus on state performance assessment programs and the lessons we can learn from their successes and failures. As noted in the chapter, too often these lessons go unheeded.

Chapter 3 explores the language of performance assessment, a domain where terminology can be ambiguous and ill defined. In this chapter, we examine the differences between the terms *performance assessment* and *performance task* and consider other vocabulary associated with these terms. In addition, the seven characteristics of complex and authentic tasks, according to Jay McTighe, are introduced in this chapter.[9]

The story of how the journey began unfolds in chapter 4. With a new strategic plan in place, district personnel sought out a means of assessing the hard-to-measure skills specified in the plan. The College and Work Readiness Assessment (CWRA) was installed as the district's annual measure of critical thinking and problem solving for high school students, and the CWRA also became the model for innovative performance tasks that were subsequently developed for the district's fourth- and seventh-grade students.

Rubric development is the topic of chapter 5. The chapter covers rubric fundamentals and provides tips on what to do and what not to do when creating rubrics. The tips are based on the author's experience conceptualizing and constructing rubrics used for scoring projects, products, and performance task responses. Although there is no one best way to develop a rubric, chapter 5 offers practical advice for tackling this essential, yet complex, process.

Chapter 6 examines the steps the district took to develop performance tasks for measuring students' proficiency in critical thinking, problem solving, and writing. As demonstrated in this chapter, designing and creating good performance tasks takes time, and every detail should be scrutinized. Our performance tasks were vetted, revised, field-tested, and reviewed and revised again, when necessary, before they were rolled out for full-scale administrations. These steps are explained in the chapter.

A major goal of scoring open-ended responses en masse is maximizing interrater agreement between scorers. Chapter 7 tells the story of how we eventually achieved this goal despite a few unplanned side trips. Consequently, the chapter includes examples of best practices—as well as some practices to avoid—for scoring performance task responses. Additionally, the advantages and disadvantages of utilizing computer scoring programs (i.e., machine scoring) are presented.

Chapter 8 comprises two sections. The first section discusses how evidence of reliability and validity was obtained for our performance tasks, and the second section examines the various ways that task results have been used by classroom teachers, schools, and the district. By the end of the chapter, readers should fully understand why deeper learning performance tasks are tests worth teaching to.

In chapter 9, Chris Gareis turns the focus to the implementation of performance assessments by teachers at the classroom level. Through examples in text and in tables, Chris defines the characteristics of different types of performance assessments, describes criteria common to all quality performance assessments, and explores research-based instructional methods that promote student engagement and deeper learning. Chapter 9 also addresses the use of performance assessments across content areas and grade levels.

We conclude with chapter 10, in which Chris argues for the widespread use of performance assessments to serve the teaching, learning, assessment, and accountability needs of schools. Through the instructive examples of the educational powerhouse of Singapore to a sampling of small, moderate-sized, and large school districts in Virginia, Chris explores the factors necessary for enacting innovative performance assessments. In addition, he spells out the characteristics needed for teacher leaders to drive this innovation.

Each chapter in this book is unique; however, taken collectively, the contents speak to both the why and how of performance tasks. Grounded in real experiences and substantiated by relevant research, the book addresses important, level-headed policies and practices of employing nontraditional means to effect deeper learning ends. We hope that by highlighting the example of one district, similar innovations will follow in schools elsewhere.

NOTES

1. Karl Fisch and Scott McLeod, "Did You Know: Shift Happens," February 8, 2007, video, 6:07, https://www.youtube.com/watch?v=ljbI-363A2Q&t=157s. Although the quote has been attributed to former secretary of education Richard Riley, Kylene Beers found no source for Riley and cited Fisch in "Sailing Over the Edge: Navigating the Uncharted Waters of a World Gone Flat," *Research in the Teaching of English* 44, no. 3 (February 2010), 352.

2. Devereux C. Josephs, "The Emerging American Scene," *The School Review* 66, no. 1 (Spring 1958), 24.

3. Colleen Flaherty, "Educators Share How No Child Left Behind Has Affected Their Classroom," *Education News*, February 20, 2015, https://educationvotes.nea.org/2015/02/20/educators-share-how-no-child-left-behind-has-affected-their-classroom.

4. Lawrence Baines, "When 'Highly Qualified' Teachers Aren't: Are We Watering Down Teacher Certification?" *Education Week*, March 7, 2017, https://www.edweek.org/ew/articles/2017/03/08/when-highly-qualified-teachers-arent.html; Harold O. Levy, "The Dumbing-down of State Testing," *Washington Post*, October 2, 2015, https://www.washingtonpost.com/opinions/the-standardized-testing-shell-game/2015/10/02/1f16c6f8-690b-11e5-9223-70cb36460919_story.html?utm_term=.d0ab414650bb; Diane Ravitch, "Time to Kill 'No Child Left Behind,'" *Education Week,* June 8, 2009, https://www.edweek.org/ew/articles/2009/06/04/33ravitch_ep.h28.html.

5. The William and Flora Hewlett Foundation is usually credited with introducing the term *deeper learning*. See Barbara Chow, "The Quest for 'Deeper Learning,'" *Education Week*, October 5, 2010, https://www.edweek.org/ew/articles/2010/10/06/06chow_ep.h30.html. However, the term was used earlier by Keith Turvey, "Towards Deeper Learning through Creativity within Online Communities in Primary Education," *Computers & Education* 46, no. 3 (April 2006), https://www.sciencedirect.com/science/article/pii/S0360131505001648.

6. Martin Luther King Jr., "The Purpose of Education," *Maroon Tiger*, February 1947, https://kinginstitute.stanford.edu/king-papers/documents/purpose-education.

7. William and Flora Hewlett Foundation, "Education: Deeper Learning," 2018, https://hewlett.org/strategy/deeper-learning.

8. *Every Student Succeeds Act*, Pub. L. No. 114-95, 129 Stat. 1802 (2015).

9. Jay McTighe, "What Is a Performance Task? (Part 1)," *Performance Task PD with Jay McTighe* (blog), April 10, 2015, *Defined Learning*, https://blog.performancetask.com/what-is-a-performance-task-part-1-9fa0d99ead3b.

Chapter 1

Teaching and Assessing for Deeper Learning

Chris Gareis

Terms such as *teaching, assessing,* and *learning* are common enough to educators and even to laypersons. When we read them, hear them, say them, or write them, we tend to know what we mean and to count on other people knowing that, too. However, one modifying word can make a difference in meaning. In the context of this book, that distinguishing word is *deeper*.

In this first chapter, we explain what we (and others) mean by the term *deeper learning*. In doing so, we explore the relevance of deeper learning to our understanding of teaching, our understanding of assessment, and our beliefs about creating coherent, innovative educational programs. Let's get started.

LEARNING

What does it mean to learn? Learning always involves change. As humans, things about us that change occur in one or more domains in which we exist and act. These are the domains of the mind, the body, and emotions. More than a half century ago, Benjamin Bloom and his colleagues operationally defined these as the cognitive domain, the psychomotor domain, and the affective domain.[1] In more recent parlance, many curriculum designers refer to knowledge, skills, and dispositions.[2]

Regardless of how we categorize it, humans think and act, and we tend to do both with purpose (sometimes with unconscious purpose, but that's not our focus here). Because these are three classic domains of human behavior, they also comprise three domains in which learning occurs: thinking, doing, and feeling.

Learning is also precipitated by experiences. You trip on a divot in the sidewalk on your daily walk from the parking lot to the front entrance of the school, and you learn to avoid the stumbling hazard. A colleague shows you how to unclog a paper jam in the copy machine, and you learn how to dislodge the offending papers on your own the next time it inevitably happens. These are changes in knowledge and skills.

Learning also occurs when dispositions change. For instance, a beloved friend passionately explains the reasons why she loves classic folk music and even entices you to listen to a few examples with her so that you can literally hear what she's talking about. You humor her at first, but then find yourself beginning to appreciate a genre of music that you had ignored (and maybe even actively avoided) for your lifetime up to that point.

Of course, learning should also occur in classrooms, so here is another example. You (as a teacher) know what you want your class of students to learn. You envision what it would look like if they could learn and make use of this thing you want them to know and be able to do. You contemplate any evidence you have of what they already know and are able to do. You consider the time and materials you have available to you. Then you plan a set of experiences for them. Perhaps you start by having them watch you do this thing you want them to be able to do. Then, you have the class try doing this thing they're learning while you watch them and provide affirmations, nudges, and outright corrections to hone their understandings. Then you have them practice it more on their own, so that their understandings are strengthened.

These experiences are a classic lesson progression: first me, then we, then you. They are learning activities. They're instruction. They're pedagogy. Regardless of what we might call them, they are *experiences* through which students' knowledge, skills, and dispositions change. Experiences—whether planned like a lesson or unplanned like tripping on a sidewalk—precipitate learning.

But learning doesn't only happen as a point in time. Learning must also persist. You need to remember that divot in the sidewalk the next day. You need to draw upon your understanding of the colored, numbered latches in the innards of the copy machine three weeks later when the darned thing freezes up again.

Whether it's the passage of a day, a week, a month, a year, or a lifetime, learning persists for some length of time. *How long* it persists is a function of many variables, of course. Two important considerations are (1) how well the learning stuck and (2) how long before I need to draw on it again. There's much more to say about that, of course, but the point here is that *if the change is fleeting, then it's not learning.* Learning is a change that persists.

Finally, learning transfers. The thing about experiences is that they happen in one time and place, but for the learning to have practical meaning, we need to be able to draw upon it in a different time and place. Returning to that divot in the sidewalk, we already know that you need to remember it the next day . . . and the next and the next, until it is repaired. But your learning from this experience can transfer to another place and even another set of circumstances. For instance, if a divot in a sidewalk is a tripping hazard, then a pothole in the road may be a driving hazard.

You might even integrate learning from multiple experiences (tripping, complex machinery, love of music) and come to the realization that driving over a pothole might not only create an uncomfortable bump during your commute but could cause a longer-term problem with your car's suspension, and you might even realize that you tend to forget about avoiding the pothole when you're listening to one of your new favorite classic folk tunes. For learning to be learning, we need to transfer it. That is, we need to make use of it in a different time, place, and set of circumstances.

Learning, then, is a change in knowledge, skills, and/or dispositions precipitated by planned and unplanned experiences, and which persists for a practical period of time and can be meaningfully applied in a time, place, and circumstance different from that in which the change originally occurred.[3] What, then, is deeper learning?

DEEPER LEARNING

The term *deeper learning* (at least in its current use in the field of education) has been credited to the William and Flora Hewlett Foundation and their launching of a major strategic initiative to reform education in the United States. Central to this reform effort is a focus on practices that equitably expand opportunities for excellence in teaching and, consequently, the manifestation of real-world outcomes for students.[4] As such, the term *deeper learning* is suggestive of both the means and the ends of education: education should be characterized by engaging, robust, meaningful learning experiences for students so that these students are best equipped for participative, constructive, fulfilling lives and careers as adults.

What, then, should characterize the means and ends of education when our aim is deeper learning? The Hewlett Foundation's seminal work on the topic in the strategy paper titled "Deeper Learning Competencies" provides a useful framework comprised of seven key features:

1. Mastering core content
2. Thinking critically
3. Solving complex problems
4. Working collaboratively

5. Communicating effectively
6. Learning how to learn
7. Developing an academic mind-set[5]

While we recommend the original work for a full explanation of the framework, we offer here our introduction to each feature.

Mastering Core Content

The term *content* is familiar enough to educators and laypersons alike, but it warrants some unpacking in relation to deeper learning. When we talk of content in schools, we typically think of the stuff of subjects, such as English, mathematics, physical education, and art. But what is the source of the *stuff* of subjects? At the risk of making too much of the point, the source of the stuff of subjects in schools is the entirety of the collective knowledge of our species! Thus, one of the main purposes of education is to convey this collective knowledge to the newest members of the human species—namely, school-aged kids—so that they don't have to go about discovering it all on their own.

Of course, we are oversimplifying things here, but the larger point remains the same: there are loads of stuff that young people *could* learn, but there is more content to learn than there is time in which to learn it. Consequently, schools need to focus teaching and learning on the content that is most essential or central to the learners—namely, the core content. As most curriculum theorists put it, an essential question in curriculum development is deciding what content is most worth knowing.[6]

But deciding *what* to teach is only a first step toward learning. One must also determine the nature and degree of learning.[7] In operationally defining deeper learning, the Hewlett Foundation summatively describes the intended nature and degree of student learning as *mastery*. Similar to other terms to which we have referred in this chapter, the term *mastery* is plain enough in meaning on the surface but warrants some explanation in the context of the notion of deeper learning. Here are two key points that we think help to illustrate the notion of mastering key content:

1. Mastery can be characterized as accurate, complete, consistent, and effective control of a body of knowledge and/or of a skill.
2. What mastery looks like is utterly dependent upon the specific knowledge or skill intended to be learned.

Let's consider two examples. First, what is mastery for an airplane pilot? Well, an indicator of mastery would be that the airplane pilot safely lands the plane in every single instance. What's more, mastery under normal circumstances is certainly the expectation, but true mastery is also exemplified in the instance of Captain Chesley "Sully" Sullenberger, who famously—and heroically—landed a commercial jet on the Hudson River in 2009 under extraordinarily challenging circumstances.

As a second example, consider mastery for professional baseball players. One important indicator of mastery is their ability to hit the ball when at bat and get on base, which is called the batting average. Among professional baseball players, an excellent batting average is about 0.300. In 2009 (the year that Captain Sully successfully landed a commercial airliner on the Hudson), the top batting average was 0.365—meaning that the top hitter in baseball could be expected to hit the ball about three out of every ten times at bat. That's a level of mastery that would never fly in the airline industry (with apologies for the pun).

Here's the point. What we mean by mastery of one set of knowledge and skills is not the same as what we mean by mastery for a different set. This is as true for landing airplanes and hitting baseballs as it is for analyzing primary sources or applying logarithmic functions. The relative expectations for mastery—for the accurate, complete, consistent, and effective use demonstration of core knowledge and skills—is a characteristic of deeper learning.

Thinking Critically

Cognition—that is, thinking—is central to learning, and the term *critical thinking* has come to be used to characterize an individual's ability to reason in a way that extends well beyond rote memorization, simple understandings, or the application of procedural skills. Critical thinking could be described as the ability to analyze novel complexities and to exercise sound reasoning and judgment to make decisions and take action. When described in such a way, thinking critically is less an academic ideal than a pragmatic imperative.

Thinking about human thinking can be, well, a tricky thing to think about! However, we have some tools available to us as educators to help us make sense of what it means to think. Perhaps most famously, Bloom and his colleagues developed a taxonomy of cognitive behaviors in the mid-twentieth century. Their intent was to develop a means by which human cognition could be categorized—and, therefore, deliberately taught and more accurately assessed—through observed student behaviors.[8]

In the original taxonomy, six levels of cognitive behaviors were identified:

1. Knowledge: recalling information
2. Comprehension: recognizing and making sense of knowledge in a novel situation
3. Application: use of knowledge and understandings

4. Analysis: examining components of a complexity
5. Synthesis: creating interrelations among complex component parts
6. Evaluation: judging the merit or worth of something

While we have provided the briefest of introductions to Bloom's taxonomy of cognitive behaviors, our main intent is to point out that critical thinking occurs when an individual is engaged in what Bloom and his colleagues would refer to as analysis, synthesis, and evaluation.

Tom Guskey, who was a student of Bloom's at the University of Chicago in the 1970s, once related this illustrative example that Bloom gave to him. Guskey shared that analysis is the ability to understand nuclear physics. Synthesis is the ability to successfully combine understandings of nuclear physics and weaponry in order to create a nuclear bomb. Evaluation is the ability to understand and wisely decide whether or not to use a nuclear bomb.[9] It's a chilling example, reflective of the era in which Bloom and his colleagues developed the taxonomy, but it makes clear the importance of critical thinking.

Bloom's taxonomy was revised in 2001, and there are other taxonomies and frameworks for representing human cognition, such as Anderson and Krathwohl's, Biggs and Collis's, and Webb et al.'s[10] In our view, none of them is perfect, but any of them can play a vitally important role in helping educators make sense of human thinking and, especially, critical thinking.

It's also important to recognize that thinking does not occur in a vacuum. To put it plainly, as humans we think about stuff . . . all kinds of stuff! We think about what our ancestors did in the past, why they did it, and what that can tell us about what we should do in the present and in the future. We think about how different species live, die, adapt, and evolve, and how the webs of species interact with each other and with the environment. We think about the origins, uses, characteristics, and adaptations of human languages. We think about how numbers are a kind of language in themselves, and we explore how that language can be used to understand anything that can be quantified, whether it's simple objects, distances, angles, or time.

These four examples are actually examples of four academic disciplines: history, biology, English, and mathematics, respectively. A discipline, in the classic sense of the word, is a branch of human knowledge and the specific methods we use to create knowledge within that branch. Returning to our examples, we use historical analysis, the scientific method, linguistics, and mathematical reasoning.

A discipline is both a branch of knowledge and a means of thinking critically to create that knowledge. Returning, then, to our explication of deeper learning, we can see that higher-order thinking and discipline-specific skills are as essential to deeper learning as mastery of core content.

Solving Complex Problems

A third defining feature of deeper learning is an emphasis on the practical use of learning, which is succinctly conveyed in the notion of solving complex problems. You might have come across one of the many versions of a cartoon that we've seen in different op-ed pages, comics, and even professional publications. A recent graduate is interviewing for a job. Across the desk is a stereotypical business executive who has just asked a question of the interviewee. On the executive's face is a flummoxed expression. The caption—the recent graduate's response to his prospective employer's question—reads something like this: "Can you give me four choices?"

The joke, of course, is a commentary on one of the unintended consequences of the high-stakes standardized testing movement and the overreliance on multiple-choice item formats.[11] The comic seems to pose the rhetorical question, "What else can we expect if we frame every problem as having one of four possible solutions?" The exasperated look on the prospective employer's face belies his experience in the "real world," where problems tend to be complex and messy . . . and where "solutions" tend to be tricky to pin down and even uncertain. Most readers of op-ed pages, the funnies, and professional journals who see a version of this cartoon get it.

You don't have to live long in the world to conclude that real life brings its share of problems and that those problems can be complex and unpredictable. The challenge, though, is to educators. How can schools integrate messy, complex problems into an institution that rightly values continuity, predictability, and stability, and which is also held to account by the public? Here are a few possible approaches that teaching for deeper learning might illuminate.

Focus on Authenticity[12]

When something is authentic, it exists somewhere on the continuum from actually being real-life to being a re-creation or reasonable facsimile of something real. For instance, a student government association in a high school that actually deliberates on issues, makes decisions, and takes actions on behalf of its constituents is authentically real. On the other hand, a model United Nations conference is a re-creation and a reasonable facsimile of international governance, but it is not a real decision-making body in and of itself. Nonetheless, authentic situations of either ilk can serve as sources of messy, complex problems for students to solve.

Consider the Present, the Future, and the Past

Authentic problems that need solving can emanate from different points in time relevant to students. For instance, what is an issue with which students contend in the present, at the age they are currently? Do fifth graders in a city school want to solve the problem of having the bare ground patch of playing area closed to them for soccer because of the derelict lot adjacent to it and its accumulation of litter, metal shards, and broken glass? That is an example of a complex, authentic problem in the present.

Could a future-oriented problem be posed to a class of seventh-grade life science students that puts them in the imagined role of officials from the Centers for Disease Control and Prevention tracking down the source of a dangerous virus? That's a scenario-based problem that potentially illustrates the relevance of seventh-grade science for students and helps them to envision a possible future career. Could a class of eleventh-grade history students research and then debate competing views regarding President Truman's decision to use the atomic bomb during World War II?

Leverage the Role of Creativity in Problem Solving

The word *creativity* is rife with meaning. It is perhaps most frequently associated with the arts, such as in describing the creativity of a painter or a writer. This is true: creativity can be manifest through aesthetics. The painter Georgia O'Keeffe, for example, painted flowers, landscapes, and other subjects using techniques and perspectives that were new and unique. As such, she opened up a novel way of interpreting and representing the world through painting. This example is not problem solving in a conventional sense but innovating in a way to create new possibilities.

Similarly, creativity can also be leveraged for problem solving when one considers that creativity is the ability to imagine a possibility and then to bring that possibility to fruition. Thus, Albert Einstein reimagined conceptions of energy, mass, and time and created a novel conceptualization of the relative relationships among them. Jeff Bezos opened himself to and explored the nascent but quickly evolving Internet. He studied and came to understand the complex world of supply chains, and he gambled on an unknown by changing the orientation of human beings toward the timeless activity of hunting and gathering (or, as we say now in the modern era, shopping). Bezos created Amazon.

Granted, O'Keeffe, Einstein, and Bezos are pretty weighty examples, but the point is that creativity is about imagining something different and useful, and then working to bring it to fruition. What's more, creativity can be aesthetic, intellectual, or entrepreneurial.

Working Collaboratively

Whereas the first three features of deeper learning are squarely focused on cognitive processes, the fourth feature accentuates the affective and social domains of human existence. More specifically, deeper learning recognizes the role of social interaction both as a means of learning and as an important outcome of learning.

The role of social interaction in learning has long been understood. We as humans are social creatures who tend to learn *with* and *from* each other in all manner of circumstances. A strong body of research suggests that teachers can leverage cooperative learning activities as a way to strengthen academic outcomes.[13]

But working collaboratively is not merely an instructional strategy. *Learning to work collaboratively* is an intended outcome in and of itself. The Partnership for 21st Century Learning identifies collaboration as one of four core skills for all humans regardless of occupation.[14] The National Research Council (NRC) identifies interpersonal competencies as an essential outcome of K–12 learning and correlates the ability to work collaboratively with positive outcomes for postsecondary education, career success, and personal health.[15] Interestingly, the NRC also contends that noncognitive outcomes (such as learning to work collaboratively) are also correlated with increased cognitive achievement in school.[16]

Communicating Effectively

Given the evidence that working collaboratively is indicative of deeper learning, so too is *communicating effectively*. Communication is, of course, the primary means through which we collaborate as humans. Language, whether spoken or written, serves to convey what is in one individual's mind to another individual's mind.

A truism of communication is that it is always two-way—that is, it always involves a sender and a receiver. Thus, communicating effectively is about learning how to speak and also learning how to listen. Communicating effectively is learning how to write and also learning how to read. Indeed, any English teacher worth his or her salt will tell you that reading and writing are two sides of the same coin, and one should wisely leverage each to teach the other. Put more succinctly, good readers tend to be good writers and good writers tend to be good readers.

But communication is not just the domain of English teachers. Again, the Partnership for 21st Century Learning identifies communication as one of the four essential competencies necessary for meaningful productivity in the present day and future.[17] Similarly, in their study of the relationship between work-and-life outcomes and K–12 education, the NRC found that intrapersonal competencies were strongly correlated with positive education, career, and health outcomes among adults. The NRC identified conscientiousness and the ability to express one's ideas and feelings, interpret the ideas and feelings of others, and respond empathetically to others as essential intrapersonal competencies.[18]

Communication is a social act and is dependent upon language. It is also important to recognize, though, that language is not only a means of communication. As humans, we also use language to create meaning. Cognitive sciences and learning theory have shown that one's language serves as a kind of filter and frame for human thinking.[19] Our language—even if "spoken" only within one's own mind—helps us to perceive, interpret, and act in the world around us. Thus, communicating effectively is also relevant to *thinking effectively*.

Learning How to Learn

As central as language is to what it means to be human, so, too, is the capacity to learn. Continuing with a theme alluded to throughout discussion of the first five characteristics of deeper learning is the premise that this characteristic—learning how to learn—is both a means to and an intended outcome of education.

Let's return for a moment to the first characteristic of deeper learning: mastering core content. A premise of this characteristic is that there is far more a student *could learn* than there is time *to learn* within the years of formal education. However, in life beyond formal schooling there will be innumerable times when one *needs* to learn—to be exposed to, grapple with, make sense of, and be able to make use of—ideas, concepts, and skills to which one was not previously exposed. In the common parlance of many a school mission statement, one needs to be equipped to be a lifelong learner.[20]

Returning to a second characteristic of deeper learning, the capacity to solve complex problems is symbiotically related to learning how to learn. Specifically, as a student develops an understanding of and ability to make use of various modes of inquiry associated with academic disciplines, the student is learning how to learn through the capacity to create new knowledge.

But the capacity for lifelong learning is not rooted in academic learning alone. Cognitive psychologists and learning theorists refer to metacognition as an innate cognitive behavior that serves to facilitate thinking and, therefore, learning.[21] In rudimentary terms, metacognition can be defined as *thinking about one's own thinking*. More specifically, metacognition serves as a kind of executive function of other modes of cognition (e.g., remembering, analyzing, evaluating).

In one sense, metacognition is an intentionality of thought, directed toward action and outcomes. Relatedly, metacognition is also relevant to the notion of a sense of one's self. Similar to the intrapersonal competencies identified in the major work-life study of the NRC, metacognition is rooted in affective dispositions such as a desire to learn and a willingness to take ownership of one's learning.

Developing an Academic Mind-Set

The seventh characteristic of deeper learning as conceptualized by the Hewlett Foundation concerns the development of a student's academic mind-set. The concept of *academic mind-set* is anchored at the intersection of cognition and affect. More specifically, it could be described as the intersection of rigorous intellectual work and motivation.

Let's face it. Learning can be difficult. If we ascribe to a definition of learning that suggests that learning is always a type of change, then it is easy to see that learning can be challenging and even off-putting at times. This challenge can be compounded in formal educational settings where students are compelled at times to study topics not of their choosing. However, the notion of academic mind-sets posits that a student's motivation, awareness of learning strategies, and willingness to persist can positively influence learning outcomes.

A study of noncognitive characteristics that can influence student learning identified academic mind-set as one significant factor. The construct has been defined as

1. a sense of belonging in a learning community,
2. a belief that effort can strengthen capacity,
3. an expectation that success can be achieved, and
4. a belief that the outcome of the work will have value.[22]

Similar to the other six characteristics of deeper learning, an academic mind-set is conceptual in nature but applied in practice. Also like the others, it is both a means and an end of education.

More specifically, though, an academic mind-set is relevant to what the NRC describes as "sophisticated disciplinary learning goals."[23] Such learning goals are multifaceted, rigorous, relevant beyond the educational setting, and anchored in authentic content and methods of the discipline. These are laudatory qualities but ones that also contribute to the inherent challenge that they present. Thus, an academic mind-set is essential to deeply learning "the skills and knowledge that students must possess to succeed in twenty-first century jobs and civic life."[24]

TEACHING FOR DEEPER LEARNING

The aims of deeper learning are for students to master core content, think critically, solve complex problems, work collaboratively, communicate effectively, direct their own learning, and persist in the face of challenges.[25] These are not only the intended outcomes of learning; they characterize the nature of learning experiences that students should experience in order to realize the intended outcomes. In other words, these seven features of deeper learning also characterize the types of methods and strategies of teaching in schools focused on deeper learning.

Indeed, in its study of work-life outcomes, the NRC found that students who attended one of a network of deeper learning high schools were significantly more likely to experience positive educational, career, and health outcomes than peer students in other schools.[26] Researchers identified a number of teaching methods associated with deeper learning, including the following:

- using multimodal representations (e.g., diagrams, flowcharts, pictures, digital images, models) to convey concepts;
- encouraging students to elaborate upon responses;
- facilitating cooperative learning experiences;
- explicitly teaching students how to pose productive questions;
- posing and then guiding students through challenging tasks; and
- using formative assessment to progress student learning.[27]

Teachers might recognize and even use some, most, or all of these exemplary instructional strategies. In fact, we find it heartening that, as a profession, we know a good deal about the kind of teaching that results in deeper learning outcomes. For example, well-known meta-analyses of empirical research on teaching and learning by Marzano and by Hattie identify specific instructional strategies that prompt communication, inquiry, analysis, evaluation, creativity, production, metacognition, and self-reflection.[28]

Research has long shown that quality teaching makes a difference in student learning.[29] What is also evident is that whether the aim is to ensure student mastery of basic knowledge and skills or to ensure the development of student capacity to engage in complex intellectual work, methods of teaching that prompt students' cognitive, physical, and affective engagement tend to be associated with stronger learning outcomes.[30]

As important as instruction is, though, our focus here is less explicitly on the types of teaching that promote deeper learning and more explicitly on the types of assessment practices that educators—that is, teachers, instructional leaders, and educational policy makers—can and should use both to promote and to provide evidence of deeper learning.

ASSESSING FOR DEEPER LEARNING

As previously alluded to, the construct of deeper learning came about in response to increasing concerns in the United States and other countries that student learning in the present day lacks both rigor and relevance.[31] Ironically, this conclusion has been widely thought to have emanated from two major efforts to achieve educational excellence, namely through the development of standards-based curriculum and high-stakes accountability.

While it is not our intention to interrogate this history exhaustively, a brief review is warranted. First, the advent of standards-based curricula in the United States is oftentimes pegged to the years immediately following an education summit attended by the nation's governors in 1989. The broad aim of the summit was to set goals and actions to strengthen public education in the United States, which included dual aims of academic excellence and equity.[32]

In the ensuing years, professional associations such as the National Council for Teachers of Mathematics and the National Council of Teachers of English created comprehensive sets of subject-based standards for student learning. In turn, these standards led to the development of comprehensive standards for K–12 public education by individual states, which largely occurred during the decade of the 1990s. A key part of the rationale was that standards-based curricula would result in more rigorous and relevant content across all schools and that the use of professional standards as a source for the development of state and even local curricula would help to ensure more equitable access to excellent educational opportunities across the country.

A second significant factor at the root of the call for deeper learning emanated from the advent of the high-stakes standardized testing movement in the early 2000s. The signature legislation dubbed No Child Left Behind mandated the creation of state-level accountability systems in which student learning was measured in English, mathematics, and science at various grade levels. In the best of lights, the broad purposes of this mandate reflected those of the standards-based movement, namely, to promote academic excellence and equity.

Arguably, these two movements have had some success in achieving their common goals. However, there have also been unintended consequences, and these consequences are associated most directly with the nature of the assessments (i.e., standardized, multiple-choice tests) used as accountability measures. For example, the high-stakes testing movement has been associated with the following:

- a narrowing of the taught curriculum to include only that which is tested and to exclude that which is not;

- a flattening of instruction to accentuate content coverage and lower-level recall; and
- an overuse of multiple-choice assessments to mimic the format of accountability tests.

Clearly, such effects are antithetical to the goals of excellence and equity, and the concern became evident among parents and students as movements to opt out of high-stakes testing swept across states in the mid-2010s.

This widespread discontent was also evident in the backlash toward the effort to develop a national curriculum known as the Common Core in the Untied States. Indeed, this was not merely consternation among disgruntled laypersons. Educational researchers came to similar conclusions. Noted experts in educational assessment Joan Herman and Robert Linn argued the following in 2014:

> History suggests that a standard-by-standard approach to teaching and learning does not work. Instead, our advice, based on research on learning, is to focus on the big ideas of what students are expected to accomplish. . . . Consider how specific standards and evidence targets can be integrated in the development and demonstration of these major competencies through appropriate performance tasks.[33]

Simply put, the types of conventional assessments used as accountability measures offer advantages such as broad content coverage, standardization of administration, and objective and efficient scoring, but they cannot assess the more authentic, complex, higher-order reasoning and problem-solving characteristics of twenty-first-century skills, career-and-college readiness, and deeper learning.

Here is another way to think of it: the term *deeper learning* begs the question, "Deeper than what?" A reasonable answer could be "Deeper than what conventional assessments are able to measure."

What, then, are such alternatives to conventional assessments? Herman and Linn refer to performance tasks. Another noted educational scholar, Linda Darling-Hammond, refers to authentic assessments, which she says "require students to develop a product, response, analysis, or problem solution that reflects the kind of reasoning or performance required beyond the classroom."[34] Others refer to performance assessments.[35]

We will clarify the terms later, but, broadly speaking, these are assessments that aim to have students draw upon a mastery of core content, think critically, and persist in their effort to solve complex problems. They are assessments that require varying degrees of student self-directedness, collaboration, and communication. In short, these types of performance tasks are intended as assessments of deeper learning.

A MEANINGFUL AND COHERENT APPROACH TO ASSESSMENT

The call to assess for deeper learning is really part of a larger call for a more meaningful and coherent approach to assessment. First, meaningful assessment is assessment that ultimately always serves to progress student learning. Some assessment practices, such as those characterized as formative, progress student learning by their very design. But we also need to ensure that our other assessments do not, at the very least, undermine student learning, such as we have seen with the unintended effects of accountability testing.

Second, meaningful assessment should be indicative of sets of knowledge, skills, and dispositions that are actually worth teachers teaching and worth students learning. For instance, we would argue that memorizing math facts is a useful thing to do. A facile recall of math facts greatly facilitates the learning of new and more complex mathematical concepts and procedures. Knowing one's math facts is also germane to making a decision to take out a loan or enjoying a successful career as an accountant. Ensuring that students learn a base of mathematical knowledge, expand and deepen their mathematical skills, and are able to apply mathematical concepts and procedures in novel, authentic situations is important.

Conventional assessments can be a quick, objective means of gauging student mastery of knowledge. We offer this one simple example to make this point: conventional assessments have their place in the classroom to assess important facts, conceptual understandings, applied methods and techniques, and analyses that are part of every academic discipline. However, as we have attempted to make clear, these types of conventional assessments need to be used in a way that is complementary to—not exclusive of—students' performance of authentic, complex tasks.

In other words, teachers should take a *balanced* approach to assessment in the classroom, making use of conventional assessments when they best serve a purpose and making use of performance assessments when they best serve another important purpose. A balanced approach to assessment also suggests making use of formative assessments as part of the act of teaching and summative assessments when need be for evaluating and sharing judgments of student learning.

Finally, we contend that not only should a balanced approach to assessment characterize assessment practices, but characterize the monitoring and accountability systems of school districts and state departments of education as well.

SUMMARY

We are heartened by the widespread and energetic movement toward teaching and assessing deeper learning. As of the time of the writing of this book, initiatives are under way in numerous schools, districts, states, provinces, and countries to articulate the deeper learning aims of K–12 schools, in terms such as critical thinking, creativity, communication, collaboration, citizenship, and wellness. Concomitantly, these innovative school, districts, states, and provinces are designing and developing performance tasks and assessments to serve as authentic, meaningful, valid, and reliable measures of deeper learning outcomes.

In this book, we provide a framework for undertaking this important work, and we illustrate it with the example of an effective, substantiated, and sustained model within one such district. Therefore, this first chapter has laid a foundation on the following takeaways:

- Student learning is the central mission of all schools, so it is important to have a clear understanding of what learning is. Succinctly stated, learning is a change in knowledge, skills, and dispositions. Learning is evident when one's knowledge, skills, and dispositions can be effectively used in a time, place, and circumstance different from that in which the learning originally occurred.
- The aim of deeper learning is for students to make use of their learning in authentic, challenging, and meaningful ways, not only as students but as young people in society and as future citizens and workers.
- Deeper learning is evident when students master core content, think critically, solve complex problems, work collaboratively, communicate effectively, direct their own learning, and persist in the face of challenges.[36]
- These are important goals, but they are not easily taught or assessed through conventional means. To teach and assess deeper learning, we need valid, reliable, meaningful, engaging performance tasks.

NOTES

1. Benjamin S. Bloom et al., ed., *Taxonomy of Educational Objectives, The Classification of Educational Goals, Handbook 1: Cognitive Domain* (New York: David McKay, 1956).

2. See, for example, Grant Wiggins and Jay McTighe, *Understanding by Design*, 2nd ed. (Alexandria, VA: Association for Supervision and Curriculum Development, 2005).

3. Christopher R. Gareis and Leslie W. Grant, *Teacher-Made Assessments: How to Connect Curriculum, Instruction, and Student Learning*, 2nd ed. (New York: Rout-

ledge, 2015); National Research Council, *Education for Life and Work: Developing Transferable Knowledge and Skills in the 21st Century* (Washington, DC: National Academies Press, 2012).

4. Siri Warkentien, Karen Charles, Laura Knapp, and David Silver, *Charting the Progress of the Hewlett Foundation's Deeper Learning Strategy 2010–2015* (Research Triangle Park, NC: Research Triangle Institute, 2017), https://hewlett.org/wp-content/uploads/2017/05/Deeper-Learning_2017_RTI-.pdf.

5. William and Flora Hewlett Foundation, "Deeper Learning Competencies," April 23, 2013, https://hewlett.org/wp-content/uploads/2016/08/Deeper_Learning_Defined__April_2013.pdf.

6. Allan C. Ornstein and Francis P. Hunkins, *Curriculum: Foundations, Principles, and Issues*, 7th ed. (Saddle River, NJ: Pearson, 2017).

7. Gareis and Grant.

8. Bloom et al.

9. Tom Guskey, personal communication, October 10, 2018.

10. Lorin W. Anderson and David R. Krathwohl, Eds., *A Taxonomy for Learning, Teaching, and Assessing: A Revision of Bloom's Taxonomy of Educational Objectives* (New York: Longman, 2001); John B. Biggs and Kevin F. Collis, *Evaluating the Quality of Learning: The SOLO Taxonomy* (New York: Academic Press, 1982); Norman L. Webb, Meredith Alt, Robert Ely, and Brian Vesperman, *Web Alignment Tool (WAT): Training manual 1.1.* (Madison: Wisconsin Center of Education Research, University of Wisconsin–Madison, 2005), http://wat.wceruw.org.

11. Gareis and Grant.

12. Chris Gareis, Stephen Geyer, and Autumn Nabors, "Assessing for Deeper Learning: How Educators Collaborated across Division Lines to Develop Performance Assessments," *Virginia ASCD Journal* 15 (Fall 2018), http://publications.catstonepress.com/i/1040708-fall-2018.

13. Robert J. Marzano, Debra J. Pickering, and Jane E. Pollock, *Classroom Instruction That Works: Research-Based Strategies for Increasing Student Achievement* (Alexandria, VA: Association for Supervision and Curriculum Development, 2001); John Hattie, *Visible Learning: A Synthesis of Over 800 Meta-Analyses Relating to Achievement* (New York: Routledge, 2009).

14. Bernie Trilling and Charles Fadel, *21st Century Skills: Learning for Life in Our Times* (San Francisco: Jossey-Bass, 2012); the Partnership for 21st Century Learning's (P21) Framework for 21st Century Learning is at http://www.battelleforkids.org/edleader21-network.

15. NRC.

16. Ibid.

17. Trilling and Fadel; P21 Framework.

18. NRC.

19. Ornstein and Hunkins; Bruce R. Joyce, Emily Calhoun, and Marsha Weil, *Models of Teaching*, 9th ed. (Boston: Pearson, 2015).

20. Christopher R. Gareis, "The Characteristics and Degrees of De Facto Consensus concerning the Mission of K–12 Public Education in Virginia" (EdD diss., College of William and Mary, 1996).

21. John H. Flavell, "Metacognition and Cognitive Monitoring: A New Area of Cognitive-Developmental Inquiry," *American Psychologist* 34, no. 10 (October 1979); Joyce, Calhoun, and Weil.

22. Camille A. Farrington et al., *Teaching Adolescents to Become Learners: The Role of Noncognitive Factors in Shaping School Performance; A Critical Literature Review* (Chicago: University of Chicago Consortium on Chicago School Research, 2012), https://consortium.uchicago.edu/sites/default/files/publications/Noncognitive%20Report.pdf.

23. NRC, 7

24. Hewlett Foundation, 1.

25. Ibid.

26. NRC.

27. Ibid.

28. Marzano, Pickering, and Pollock; Hattie.

29. William L. Sanders and Sandra L. Horn, "Research Findings from the Tennessee Value-Added Assessment System (TVAAS) Database: Implications for Educational Evaluation and Research," *Journal of Personnel Evaluation in Education* 12, no. 3 (September 1998); James H. Stronge, *Qualities of Effective Teachers*, 2nd ed. (Alexandria, VA: Association for Supervision and Curriculum Development, 2007).

30. Fred M. Newman, Anthony S. Bryk, and Jenny K. Nagoaka, *Authentic Intellectual Work and Standardized Tests: Conflict or Coexistence?* (Chicago: Consortium on Chicago School Research, 2001), https://consortium.uchicago.edu/sites/default/files/publications/p0a02.pdf.

31. Barbara R. Blackburn, *Rigor Is NOT a Four-Letter Word* (New York: Routledge, 2013).

32. Alyson Klein, "Historic Sit-Down Propelled National Drive for Standards-Based Accountability," *Education Week,* September 23, 2014, https://www.edweek.org/ew/articles/2014/09/24/05summit.h34.html.

33. Joan Herman and Robert Linn, "New Assessments, New Rigor," *Educational Leadership* 71, no. 6 (March 2014), 34.

34. Linda Darling-Hammond and Frank Adamson, *Beyond the Bubble Test: How Performance Assessments Support 21st Century Learning* (San Francisco: Jossey-Bass, 2014), 12.

35. Christopher R. Gareis, "Exploring the Intersectionality of Performance Assessments: Crossroads, Crosswords, and Crosshairs" (keynote presentation, 27th Annual Conference of the Consortium for Research on Educational Assessment and Teaching Effectiveness, Williamsburg, VA, October 11, 2018).

36. Ibid.

Chapter 2

Looking Back at Performance Assessment

A solid understanding of prior initiatives and outcomes in any discipline offers invaluable perspectives for individuals and groups within the discipline. It allows them to navigate forward while avoiding the mistakes of the past. Like many educational concepts and rock bands from the previous century, performance assessment has made a comeback, though the same concerns and problems related to this type of assessment remain.

Chapter 2 recaps federal and state education policy during the past thirty-five years, primarily focusing on large-scale standardized testing and statewide performance assessment programs. The lessons learned from earlier endeavors into the realm of performance assessment should serve to inform later, similar initiatives, yet this is not always the case. Examining these endeavors provides a suitable backdrop for the rest of this book.

THE ROOTS OF MODERN EDUCATIONAL REFORM

"Our once unchallenged preeminence in commerce, industry, science, and technological innovation is being overtaken by competitors throughout the world."[1] This is not a recent warning—it is the opening salvo of *A Nation at Risk*, a scathing report released in April 1983 by President Reagan's National Commission on Excellence in Education. The full title of the report is *A Nation at Risk: The Imperative for Educational Reform*. Many consider it to be the jumping-off point of the modern educational reform movement, efforts that continue to this day.

Some scholars have suggested Reagan's commission got it wrong in *A Nation at Risk*, due in part to faulty methodology. Most of the report's "Indicators of the Risk" were results from standardized, multiple-choice tests and other assessments comprising mainly multiple-choice questions, including the National Assessment of Educational Progress (NAEP) and the Scholastic Aptitude Test (SAT). The so-called Sandia Report, completed in 1991, reexamined the data and concluded there were "steady or slightly improving trends" on almost every measure used as an indicator.[2]

Nonetheless, the public's belief that our schools were failing was an affront to our national pride. The time was ripe for educational reform. Most states welcomed reform because it translated to more federal funding for education. States quickly created their own commissions and task forces to evaluate existing educational policies and make recommendations. The 1980s became known as the reform decade, as an unprecedented wave of new policies meant to fix public education were introduced.[3]

Numerous bills enacted into law called for increased testing, seen as the best way to gauge the success or failure of reform attempts. In some states, students as young as first graders were required to take standardized, multiple-choice tests. The public approved of this surge in high-stakes testing, a term that came into vogue during the reform decade. High-stakes testing means that test results are used to make important decisions, such as promotion to the next grade level.[4] The support among Americans for testing was quite strong, with 77 percent backing the idea of a national standardized test.[5]

Absent a national test, the majority of states administered commercially produced, nationally normed tests. The most popular tests were the California Achievement Test (CAT), the Comprehensive Test of Basic Skills (CTBS), the Iowa Test of Basic Skills (ITBS), the Metropolitan Achievement Test, 6th Edition (MAT-6), and the Stanford Achievement Test, 7th Edition (SAT-7). These were exclusively or predominantly multiple-choice tests. Eighteen states allowed local districts to select their own assessments—many chose the CAT, CTBS, ITBS, MAT-6, or SAT-7—while a few states developed their own tests for districts to administer.[6]

THE STAGE IS SET FOR PERFORMANCE ASSESSMENT

In the late 1980s, a remarkable discovery appeared in a brief report published by an obscure organization, Friends for Education. The report, *Nationally Normed Elementary Achievement Testing in America's Public Schools: How All Fifty States Are Above the National Average*, revealed that all fifty states maintained that their elementary students had scored above the norm on a state-mandated, standardized test.[7]

The *Lake Wobegon effect*, named for a mythical town where all children are above average, occurred in approximately 90 percent of the school districts in the United States. The inflated scores were attributed primarily to outdated or inaccurate test norms and the practice of teaching to the test.[8] The second explanation should come as no surprise. When high-stakes test results are publicized, teaching to the test—or teaching questions on the test—becomes more common than educators would care to admit.

By the early 1990s, concerns about the increase in accountability testing and its effect on students and teachers became widespread. People began to seriously question the value of standardized, multiple-choice tests. Accordingly, Congress commissioned a lengthy report, *Testing in American Schools: Asking the Right Questions*, which reiterated the Lake Wobegon findings. The report also cited extensive research documenting the unintended consequences of high-stakes testing, including a lack of correspondence between gains in student learning and test scores gains, as well as instructional emphasis on basic skills instead of higher-order thinking skills.[9]

Testing in American Schools devoted a full chapter to performance assessment, pointing out two critical features of this type of assessment: "They involve direct observation of student behavior on tasks resembling those considered necessary in the real world, and they shed light on students' learning and thinking processes."[10] At the time the report was released, the standards-based reform movement in education had already taken root.

The standards-based movement advocated for replacing traditional, rote instruction with teaching aligned to more rigorous standards, which some experts referred to as a "thinking curriculum."[11] Like the reform initiatives of the 1980s, the standards movement relied in large part on state and district-wide accountability tests to measure student attainment of the new standards. Unlike the accountability tests of the 1980s, standards-based assessments included portfolios, hands-on tasks, open-ended test questions, and other kinds of performance assessment.

THE CHALLENGES OF LARGE-SCALE PERFORMANCE ASSESSMENT

By 1992, the majority of states employed some type of performance assessment, though most of them were writing assessments. California, Kentucky, Maryland, and Vermont were just a few states whose performance assessment programs were designed to measure standards-based reforms in multiple content areas. This section focuses on the challenges these states faced in implementing performance assessment.

All four assessment programs—the California Learning Assessment System (CLAS), the Kentucky Instructional Results Information System

(KIRIS), the Maryland School Performance Assessment System (MSPAS), and the Vermont Portfolio Assessment Program—were initiated between 1991 and 1993. Although the programs each had unique aspects, they were all costly and experienced many of the same problems. Kentucky's and Vermont's programs were part of state educational investments that cost over $500 million apiece.[12]

Portfolio assessment was the mainstay of Vermont's program. The program was made up of writing and mathematics portfolios compiled by fourth- and eighth-grade students. The portfolios were supplemented by a writing prompt and a math test that comprised mostly multiple-choice questions.[13] The initial Vermont Portfolio Assessment Program was nothing spectacular, but it took three years to develop.

The writing and math portfolio assessments of California's CLAS and Kentucky's KIRIS were also intended for students in grades 4 and 8. Scoring concerns dominated discussions related to portfolio assessments. The Vermont writing portfolio was hindered by various factors. There was an abundance of teachers waiting to be trained to use the rubrics, which were later seen as inferior products. Additionally, interrater agreement between teachers who underwent training was quite low.[14] In California, state-appointed committees and the press viewed the scoring process for CLAS portfolio assessments as lacking objectivity.[15]

Kentucky recognized possible scoring issues early and went to work on strengthening their rubrics and portfolio scorer training programs. By the mid-1990s, a respectable 77 percent agreement rate between scorers was reported for KIRIS writing portfolios. Despite this, Kentucky had troubles of its own. Assembling the portfolios was considered burdensome and stakeholders suspected the possibility of scoring bias.[16]

CLAS, KIRIS, and the performance assessment programs of Vermont and Maryland each included writing prompts. Depending on the state, students wrote relatively short answers, essays, or both. A number of writing prompts were tainted from the start. The KIRIS, for instance, contained constructed-response questions judged to be "far too difficult for students to even begin to make a response."[17]

Another review committee called into question certain content on Maryland's MSPAS, but the CLAS achieved the dubious honor of having America's most contentious test items and writing prompts. Soon after the first administration of the CLAS in 1993, the California controversy commenced. Among other problems, many parents claimed parts of the assessment were too subjective and invaded students' privacy.[18] As expected, the media fueled the fire.

A 1994 article in the *Los Angeles Times* reported Orange County high school students' opinions about CLAS. One sophomore said, "I felt that some of the questions intruded into my life. They seemed like personal questions, and it made me feel uncomfortable answering them. Even though the reader-grader of the test would not know me, I still felt violated and found myself making up answers for the essays. It seemed pointless."[19]

Ultimately, every performance assessment program described in this section was dismantled. Amid the hoopla about its intrusiveness, the Golden State's CLAS was the first to go. CLAS was short-lived—development began in 1990 and its demise occurred in 1994.[20] After much political and public debate, Kentucky's KIRIS was replaced in 1998 by the Commonwealth Assessment Test System (CATS). Although CATS retained the writing portfolio and some constructed-response items, the Kentucky legislature removed the term *performance assessment* when KIRIS gave way to CATS.[21] Maryland's MSPAS and the Vermont Portfolio Assessment Program both lasted longer, into the early years of the No Child Left Behind (NCLB) era.[22]

The California, Kentucky, Maryland, and Vermont performance assessment programs were all flawed to different degrees, yet they included commendable attempts to gauge students' higher-order thinking skills, or deeper learning, as it is commonly called today. Various reports and articles examining these and other innovative assessment programs of the 1990s are readily available; several are listed in the notes at the end of this chapter.

INTO THE NEW MILLENNIUM

In 1989, a coalition of governors proposed a program that set lofty goals for American public education. The Goals 2000: Educate America Act was signed into law five years later with strong support from both sides of the aisle. Of the eight goals, some required substantial resources but lacked funding, while others would be impossible to attain by the year 2000 (e.g., "All children in America will start school ready to learn"; "Every school in the United States will be free of drugs, violence, and the unauthorized presence of firearms and alcohol and will offer a disciplined environment conducive to learning"). Not one goal was met by the turn of the century.[23]

Goals 2000 did, however, focus on the achievement of individual students. Goals 2000's successor, the bipartisan NCLB, required states to test every student in grades 3–8 annually. With its emphasis on high-stakes accountability testing, NCLB transformed the standards-based reform movement into what some experts called test-based reform, or "a system in which educators and others rely primarily on the test rather than the standards to communicate expectations and to inform practice."[24]

This system was more stick than carrot and involved a considerable amount of federal money. By tying Title I funds to NCLB's accountability requirements, the feds got the full attention of states. Money also influenced the decision to discontinue almost every state's performance assessment program. Large-scale performance assessment, seen as costly and time-consuming, yielded to cheaper multiple-choice tests that were easier to administer and score. In many states, meaningful instruction and assessment in science, social studies, and the arts—content areas that have traditionally embraced performance assessment—were placed on the back burner due to NCLB's concentration on reading and math scores.

Seven years into the NCLB era, governors and educational leaders from forty-eight states, two territories, and the District of Columbia (DC) began an initiative "to ensure all students, regardless of where they live, are graduating high school prepared for college, career, and life."[25] The promise of this initiative, known as the Common Core State Standards (CCSS), was a set of state and internationally benchmarked standards in English language arts (ELA) and mathematics, along with high-quality summative assessments fully aligned with the standards.

In 2010, the US Department of Education awarded $330 million to two consortia to develop the CCSS assessments. The combined membership of the consortia—Partnership for Assessment of Readiness for College and Careers (PARCC) and Smarter Balanced Assessment Consortium (SBAC)—comprised forty-six states and DC. Performance tasks and constructed-response items delivered online were key components of both the PARCC and SBAC assessments.

Unfortunately, problems plagued the assessments and their parent consortia. From 2013 to 2017, over thirty states reported technical glitches.[26] There were also disagreements between states and consortia concerning who was in charge of proficiency standards and the tests.[27] In some states, political battles waged over test-related technology expenses and the unending fight over federal versus state control of public education. Teachers, parents, and students complained about the length of the tests; New York and a few other states saw countless students opt out of CCSS tests.[28] By 2018, only twenty states were participating in PARCC and SBAC.

CONTEMPORARY EDUCATIONAL ASSESSMENT

Despite the consortia's ongoing struggles, their assessment enterprises have had positive aftereffects. The CCSS called for high-quality formative and summative assessments that fully supported the standards, which were "aligned with college and career expectations [and] based on rigorous content and application of knowledge through higher-order thinking skills."[29] This challenge was met by PARCC and SBAC with state-of-the-art assessments delivered online. The consortia's efforts helped bring large-scale testing into the twenty-first century.

The ripple effect from advances in testing meant states could no longer justify the sole use of standardized, multiple-choice tests to meet federal testing requirements. To address the issue of measuring deeper learning, most of the non-CCSS and former CCSS states started contracting with vendors (e.g., American Institutes for Research, Measured Progress, Pearson) to customize summative assessments or administer the vendor's product. Several states generated hybrid tests that include questions from PARCC or SBAC item banks.[30]

America's most recent federal education legislation, the Every Student Succeeds Act (ESSA), went into full effect for the 2018–2019 school year. Although ESSA retained many of NCLB's testing regulations—for example, mandated ELA and math testing of students in grades 3–8—the law allowed a bit of flexibility and incentive for states to improve testing practices. Up to seven states were permitted to apply for grant money to develop large-scale performance assessments. By the April 2018 deadline, however, only Louisiana, New Hampshire, and Puerto Rico had applied to be part of ESSA's innovative assessment pilot program.[31]

SUMMARY

This chapter reviewed educational reforms and K–12 state-level testing from the 1980s through 2018, with special attention on performance assessments. Here are a few historical takeaways:

- Developing large-scale performance assessments is much costlier and more time-consuming than implementing a multiple-choice assessment program.
- Scoring any type of performance assessment with a rubric is a fundamentally subjective process.
- Carefully reviewing performance assessments and prompts in advance can avert serious problems later.

One takeaway not mentioned mirrors the words of philosopher George Santayana: "Those who cannot remember the past are condemned to repeat it."[32] Too often, educators launch an initiative without checking to see if something similar had been tried previously. These well-intentioned initiatives are sometimes just rebranded versions of earlier endeavors. Given the availability of educational research and other information, educators who are considering a new venture should begin by doing their homework.

NOTES

1. National Commission on Excellence in Education, *A Nation at Risk: The Imperative for Educational Reform* (Washington, DC: US Government Printing Office, 1983), 1.
2. Charles C. Carson, Robert M. Huelskamp, and Thomas D. Woodall, "Perspectives on Education in America: An Annotated Briefing, April 1992," *The Journal of Educational Research* 86, no. 5 (May–June 1993), 259.
3. William A. Firestone, Sheila Rosenblum, Beth D. Bader, and Diane Massell, *Education Reform from 1983 to 1990: State Action and District Response* (New Brunswick, NJ: Consortium for Policy Research in Education, 1991), 60, https://files.eric.ed.gov/fulltext/ED342077.pdf.
4. *Glossary of Education Reform*, s.v. "High-Stakes Test," last updated August 8, 2014, https://www.edglossary.org/high-stakes-testing.
5. Alec M. Gallup, *The 18th Annual Gallup Poll of the Public's Attitudes toward the Public Schools* (Bloomington, IN: Phi Delta Kappa Research Foundation, 1986), 10.
6. John J. Cannell, *Nationally Normed Elementary Achievement Testing in America's Public Schools: How All Fifty States Are Above the National Average* (Daniels, WV: Friends for Education, 1987).
7. Ibid.
8. Robert L. Linn, M. Elizabeth Graue, and Nancy M. Sanders, "Comparing State and District Test Results to National Norms: Interpretations of Scoring 'Above the National Average'" (paper presented at the Annual Meeting of the American Educational Research Association, San Francisco, CA, March 27–31, 1989), 32.
9. US Congress, Office of Technology Assessment, *Testing in American Schools: Asking the Right Questions* (Washington, DC: U.S. Government Printing Office, 1992), 63–64.
10. Ibid., 201.
11. Lauren B. Resnick and Daniel P. Resnick, "Assessing the Thinking Curriculum: New Tools for Educational Reform," in *Changing Assessment: Alternative Views of Aptitude, Achievement, and Instruction*, ed. Bernard R. Gifford and Mary Catherine O'Connor (Boston: Kluwer, 1992), 38.
12. Ruth Chung Wei, Raymond L. Pecheone, and Katherine L. Wilczak, *Performance Assessment 2.0: Lessons from Large-Scale Policy and Practice* (Stanford, CA: Stanford University, 2014), 28, https://scale.stanford.edu/sites/default/files/Performance%20Assessment%202.0%20Final_Digital.pdf.
13. Brian Stecher, *Performance Assessment in an Era of Standards-Based Educational Accountability* (Stanford, CA: Stanford University, Stanford Center for Opportunity Policy in Education, 2010), 12, https://scale.stanford.edu/system/files/performance-assessment-era-standards-based-educational-accountability.pdf.
14. Daniel Koretz, Brian Stecher, Stephen Klein, and Daniel McCaffrey, "The Vermont Portfolio Assessment Program: Findings and Implications," *Educational Measurement: Issues and Practice* 13, no. 3 (September 1994), 5–10.
15. Stecher, 17.

16. Ibid., 14.

17. George K. Cunningham, "Learning from Kentucky's Failed Accountability System," in *Testing Student Learning, Evaluating Teaching Effectiveness*, ed. Williamson M. Evers and Herbert J. Walberg (Stanford, CA: Hoover Institution Press, 2004), 273.

18. Wei, Pecheone, and Wilczak, 37.

19. *Los Angeles Times*, "OC High Asks: What's Your Opinion of the CLAS (California Learning Assessment System) Tests? Should They Continue?" May 20, 1994, http://articles.latimes.com/1994-05-20/news/ls-60066_1_california-learning-assessment-system.

20. Laura S. Hamilton, Brian M. Stecher, and Kun Yuan, *Standards-Based Reform in the United States: History, Research, and Future Directions* (Santa Monica, CA: RAND Corporation, 2008), 25, https://www.rand.org/pubs/reprints/RP1384.html.

21. Cunningham, 250.

22. Wei, Pecheone, and Wilczak, 7.

23. Richard Rothstein, "'Goals 2000' Scorecard: Failure Pitches a Shutout," Economic Policy Institute, December 22, 1999, https://www.epi.org/publication/webfeat_lessons19991222.

24. Hamilton, Stecher, and Yuan, 29.

25. Common Core State Standards Initiative, "About the Standards," 2018, http://www.corestandards.org/about-the-standards.

26. National Center for Fair and Open Testing, "U.S. Computerized Testing Problems: Chronology," updated April 24, 2018, http://fairtest.org/computerized-testing-problems-chronology.

27. Jaekyung Lee and Yin Wu, "Is the Common Core Racing America to the Top? Tracking Changes in State Standards, School Practices, and Student Achievement," *Education Policy Analysis Archives*, 25, no. 35 (April 10, 2017), 3.

28. Elizabeth A. Harris, "As Tests Begin, Chancellor Comes Out against 'Opt Out,'" *New York Times*, April 18, 2018, https://www.nytimes.com/2018/04/10/nyregion/tests-chancellor-carranza-nyc-opt-out.html.

29. Common Core State Standards Initiative.

30. Education Commission of the States, "50-State Comparison: State Summative Assessments—Math and English Language Arts Assessments and Vendors for Grades 3–8 (2017–18)," April 2018, http://ecs.force.com/mbdata/mbquestrt?rep=SUM1801.

31. Alyson Klein, "Louisiana, New Hampshire, and Puerto Rico Apply for ESSA Innovative Testing Pilot," *Politics K–12* (blog), *Education Week*, April 3, 2018, https://blogs.edweek.org/edweek/campaign-K–12/2018/04/ESSA_testing_pilot_louisiana_new_hampshire_and_puerto_rico.html.

32. George Santayana, *The Life of Reason: The Phases of Human Progress*, Vol. 1 (New York: C. Scribner's Sons, 1905; New York: Dover, 1980), 172. Citation refers to the Dover edition.

Chapter 3

Performance Assessment versus Performance Tasks

Much of the discussion in the previous chapter centered on performance assessment in general. Now we direct our attention toward performance tasks. While many people believe the terms *performance assessment* and *performance task* are synonymous, they are not. This brief chapter establishes a common understanding of these terms and describes the characteristics of deeper learning performance tasks. In addition to defining performance assessment and performance task, we examine several related expressions.

THE JARGON OF PERFORMANCE ASSESSMENT

Terminology is in the eye of the beholder. Laypersons might not distinguish between two terms and thus use them interchangeably. Conversely, experts recognize the differences between the same pair of terms, even when the differences are subtle. Not only are the terms *performance assessment* and *performance task* swapped freely with each other, additional words and phrases are often substituted for them. Here are a few terms found in the literature that have similar, sometimes indistinguishable, meanings as performance assessment:

- Alternative assessment
- Authentic assessment
- Authentic performance assessment
- Performance-based assessment, or PBA

Instead of defining each term and explaining what may or may not be significant differences between the terms, let's start with a rudimentary definition of performance assessment. As stated by the *Standards for Educational and Psychological Testing*, a performance assessment is an assessment "for which the test taker actually demonstrates the skills the test is intended to measure by doing the tasks that require those skills."[1]

The circularity of the *Standards* definition is an implicit reference to validity. Educational researchers and measurement authorities—as well as people who paid attention in their assessment classes—understand that validity is critical. Validity addresses this question: does the assessment measure what it's supposed to measure? It is indeed of paramount importance for any assessment.

Another definition of performance assessment appeared in a 2015 white paper by Ace Parsi and Linda Darling-Hammond. The paper's audience was state boards of education, so the authors made a clear distinction between multiple-choice tests and performance assessment. The latter was defined as "assessments that require students to craft their own responses to problems through constructing an answer, producing a product, or performing an activity rather than merely selecting from multiple-choice answers."[2]

Two terms on the short list at the beginning of this section start with the word *authentic*. Many people do not differentiate between authentic assessment and performance assessment; others argue that unless an assessment possesses a high degree of fidelity to the skill being measured, it cannot be considered authentic.[3] One researcher who analyzed literature from the debate reported that authentic assessment and performance assessment "have both been given a number of different meanings and unclear definitions and are in some publications not defined at all."[4]

Grant Wiggins and Jay McTighe, the authors of the seminal *Understanding by Design* (*UbD*), noted that students' understanding of concepts could be revealed through the use of authentic performance tasks. To be authentic, according to *UbD*, performance tasks need to involve real-life contexts and replicate challenging scenarios that are somewhat unstructured, such as situations adults encounter every day. Furthermore, the tasks require students to skillfully use knowledge to effectively perform the work necessary to address the challenges. The products of authentic tasks allow for the holistic assessment of students' knowledge, skills, and judgment, rather than the assessment of "isolated bits of knowledge or elements of performance."[5] The performance tasks at the heart of this book meet these requirements.

Wiggins and McTighe also asserted that performance assessment is more than just a one-shot deal. In *UbD*, they wrote, "performance assessment involves more than a single test of performance and might use other modes of assessment as well."[6] In other words, performance assessment comprises multiple measures. An example is portfolio assessment. Portfolios contain an array of student work samples that provide evidence of proficiency in a course or subject. Although performance assessment is usually thought of as a lone activity, project, or task, it can cover different products over a period of time.

THE PREPONDERANCE OF PERFORMANCE TASKS

Performance assessment comes in a variety of types. Another search through the literature resulted in a list of twenty-one terms, shown in table 3.1. These activities and products are not exclusive of each other—a few terms are fundamentally identical in meaning. What they have in common is they are all activities that ask for students to demonstrate a skill, knowledge, or both skills and knowledge.

Readers may have noticed that performance task is included in table 3.1. For the purposes of this book, we view performance tasks as a type of performance assessment. Jay McTighe gave us an appropriate definition of performance task: "A performance task is any learning activity or assessment that asks students to *perform* to demonstrate their knowledge, understanding and proficiency. Performance tasks yield a tangible product and/or performance that serve as evidence of learning."[7]

Individuals who have explored the vast range of performance tasks—available online from vendors, nonprofit organizations, state departments of education, school districts, teacher websites, and other sources—know that tasks come in various shapes, sizes, and difficulty levels. A math problem that requires students to perform an operation and then fill in the blank is an example of a rudimentary performance task. Word problems are also performance tasks. In reading, the most basic performance tasks are short passages, sometimes a single sentence, followed by a question.

If the modest tasks just described—the math problem or the short reading passage—provided options for students to select the correct answer, would they still be considered performance tasks? The majority of educators would

Table 3.1 Types of performance assessments

• computer-based simulation	• on-demand task	• problem solution
• demonstration	• original creation	• product
• document-based question	• performance exercise	• project
• essay	• performance task	• report
• extended-response question	• performance test	• research task
• inquiry task	• portfolio	• restricted-response question
• investigation	• presentation	• writing prompt

probably say no, which would be in line with one definition of performance assessment given earlier: "assessments that require students to craft their own responses . . . rather than merely selecting from multiple-choice answers."[8]

But multiple-choice questions are in fact included within the scope of performance tasks. A number of sample performance task items are accessible on the website of the Smarter Balanced Assessment Consortium (SBAC). After clicking on a task item, a window pops up with the message, "Note about ELA [or Math] Performance Task Items—The item you selected is part of a Performance Task, which consists of multiple items of different types (for example, Multiple Choice, Short Answer, Extended Response, etc.)."[9]

With a multi-item approach to performance task structure, SBAC seems to concur with the *UbD* interpretation of performance assessment, as their tasks have "more than a single test of performance and might use other modes of assessment."[10] On the website of the Partnership for Assessment of Readiness for College and Careers (PARCC), multiple-choice questions can be found among the released PARCC writing tasks.

CHARACTERISTICS OF DEEPER LEARNING TASKS

In chapter 1, Chris Gareis explained the concept of deeper learning and called for a meaningful and coherent approach to assessment. The inclusion of performance tasks within a balanced system of accountability can serve to both measure and advance deeper learning. At this time, we again turn to Jay McTighe for more detail on what performance tasks for measuring deeper learning look like.

Jay presented seven characteristics of performance tasks (see textbox 3.1). The first two characteristics tell us that performance tasks are open ended and require higher-order thinking. Obviously, a student must think more deeply to create a response as opposed to choosing a predetermined best answer. Characteristics 3, 5, and 6 reflect the engaging, intricate nature of effective performance tasks. The fourth characteristic refers to a student's ability to apply deeper learning within given circumstances. The last characteristic emphasizes the importance of incorporating rubrics, the topic of chapter 5. Similar to *UbD*'s requirements for authentic tasks, the characteristics in textbox 3.1 correspond with the features of the performance tasks described in upcoming chapters.

Textbox 3.1
CHARACTERISTICS OF PERFORMANCE TASKS

1. Performance tasks call for the application of knowledge and skills, not just recall or recognition.
2. Performance tasks are open-ended and typically do not yield a single, correct answer.
3. Performance tasks establish novel and authentic contexts for performance.
4. Performance tasks provide evidence of understanding via transfer.
5. Performance tasks are multifaceted.
6. Performance tasks can integrate two or more subjects as well as 21st century skills.
7. Performances on open-ended tasks are evaluated with established criteria and rubrics.

Used with permission from Jay McTighe.

SUMMARY

The terms *performance assessment* and *performance task* were defined and differentiated in this chapter. From our perspective, all performance tasks are performance assessments, but not all performance assessments are performance tasks. In the broadest sense of the term, a performance task can be any assessment in which students generate an answer, produce a product, or perform an activity to demonstrate a skill or knowledge.

Performance tasks designed to measure deeper learning are complex. It becomes increasingly apparent in our book that creating these tasks is demanding work. The work calls for deeper learning skills—such as critical thinking and problem solving—from the designers themselves. Educators interested in developing deeper learning performance tasks should note two takeaways from this chapter:

- Compared with contrived assessments and simple performance tasks, authentic tasks that replicate challenging situations from everyday life are a better and more engaging means for students to demonstrate their knowledge and judgment.
- Effective deeper learning tasks are open ended and multifaceted; they require students to apply the actual skills being assessed.

NOTES

1. American Educational Research Association, American Psychological Association, and National Council for Measurement in Education, *Standards for Educational and Psychological Testing* (Washington, DC: American Educational Research Association, 2014), 221.

2. Ace Parsi and Linda Darling-Hammond, *Performance Assessments: How State Policy Can Advance Assessments for 21st Century Learning* (Arlington, VA: National Association of State Boards of Education, 2015), 3, http://www.nasbe.org/wp-content/uploads/Performance-Assessment-white-paper.pdf.

3. Judith T. M. Gulikers, Theo J. Bastiaens, and Paul A. Kirschner, "Perceptions of Authentic Assessment: Five Dimensions of Authenticity" (paper presented at the Second Biannual Joint Northumbria/European Association for Research on Learning and Instruction SIG Assessment Conference, Bergen, Norway, 2014), 4.

4. Torulf Palm, "Performance Assessment and Authentic Assessment: A Conceptual Analysis of the Literature," *Practical Assessment, Research & Evaluation* 13, no. 4 (April 2008), 1, https://pareonline.net/getvn.asp?v=13&n=4.

5. Grant Wiggins and Jay McTighe, *Understanding by Design,* 2nd ed. (Alexandria, VA: Association for Supervision and Curriculum Development, 2005), 153–54.

6. Ibid., 346.

7. Jay McTighe, "What Is a Performance Task? (Part 1)," *Performance Task PD with Jay McTighe* (blog), April 10, 2015, *Defined Learning,* https://blog.performancetask.com/what-is-a-performance-task-part-1-9fa0d99ead3b.

8. Parsi and Hammond, 3.

9. Smarter Balanced Assessment Consortium, "Sample Items," accessed July 31, 2019, http://sampleitems.smarterbalanced.org/BrowseItems.

10. Wiggins and McTighe, 346.

Chapter 4

Embarking upon the Journey

Deeper learning prepares students for the future by implementing a rigorous curriculum and lessons that involve essential skills and knowledge. As noted in chapter 1, the William and Flora Hewlett Foundation's deeper learning framework comprises seven competencies: mastering core content, thinking critically, solving complex problems, working collaboratively, communicating effectively, learning how to learn, and developing an academic mind-set.[1]

At present, school districts across the country have mission statements, vision statements, strategic goals, key initiatives, and so on that allude to deeper learning competencies and deeper learning's fundamental purposes. Statements such as "Every student graduates with the skills needed to compete in the 21st century"[2] and "Through both critical thinking and problem solving instructional practices, our students will be prepared for success in life after graduation"[3] appear on the websites of many school districts, large and small alike.

Year after year, hardworking educators take on the challenge of planning and delivering instruction to foster their students' skills in critical thinking, problem solving, and other deeper learning competencies. But is teaching the skills enough? How can educators find out whether their students are acquiring the skills? And how can educators differentiate between students who have mastered the skills and those who need additional help? Chapter 4 describes the beginning of a journey that one school system took to answer these questions.

A STRATEGY FOR THE FUTURE

Years before the Hewlett Foundation defined deeper learning, a large school district in Virginia adopted a strategic plan to address most of the competencies that were identified later in the Hewlett definition. According to the plan, Compass to 2015, the primary focus of Virginia Beach City Public Schools (VBCPS) would be on "teaching and assessing those skills our students need to thrive as twenty-first-century learners, workers, and citizens."[4] The skills included academic proficiency, critical thinking, problem solving, independent learning, and effective communication and collaboration.

Unlike the strategic plans of many other school districts, Compass to 2015 emphasized both teaching *and* assessing. To bolster the assessment component, one strategic objective was to implement an assessment system for monitoring students' progress on the identified skills. This was somewhat of a concern for the VBCPS Office of Student Assessment, whose main responsibility was overseeing the administration of state-mandated and districtwide tests, the multiple-choice tests that gauged our students' mastery of core content (i.e., academic proficiency). The concern was how to summatively assess critical thinking, problem solving, and other hard-to-measure skills specified in our new strategic plan.

AN ASSESSMENT TO EMULATE

We were fortunate that Tony Wagner—author, scholar, and founder of Harvard's Change Leadership Group—served as a consultant to VBCPS during the development of Compass to 2015. When the topic of assessing higher-order competencies came up, Wagner told us about the College and Work Readiness Assessment (CWRA), an innovative performance task for high school students. The CWRA measured analytic reasoning and evaluation, problem solving, writing effectiveness, and writing mechanics. These skills paralleled three of our strategic plan's outcomes for student success: critical thinking, problem solving, and effective communication.

The Council for Aid to Education (CAE), a nonprofit organization "committed to helping education institutions measure and improve learning outcomes by offering innovative assessments and developing custom tests,"[5] created the CWRA and its predecessor, the Collegiate Learning Assessment (CLA), which was designed for college students. Secondary and undergraduate students across the nation and internationally continue to take enhanced versions of the assessments, the CWRA+ and the CLA+.

The CLA was conceptualized in the early 2000s. At the time, colleges and universities were facing decades of pressure to demonstrate accountability for their students' learning. Grade point averages were not seen as an adequate measure. In 2005, a group of researchers published the results of a study in which large samples of students at different colleges were given, among other tests, performance tasks designed to assess critical-thinking skills.[6]

The performance tasks developed by the researchers expanded upon an idea they borrowed from the bar exam. The bar exam's performance test section presents real-world legal situations that examinees might encounter as lawyers. Similarly, each of the performance tasks created by the researchers included a realistic problem and various documents. Students in the study reviewed the situation, analyzed the documents, and then wrote a mock memo to address the problem.

The results of the study—relative to the performance tasks—indicated that

- scoring the performance task responses was reliable;
- there was a high correlation (.84) between responses scored by computer and human raters; and
- students found the tasks interesting and engaging.[7]

The results demonstrated that a sophisticated performance task, administered on a large scale, could be scored reliably at a reasonable cost. Furthermore, performance tasks involving hypothetical yet realistic situations were intrinsically motivating, which suggested that most students put forth their best effort. By the time the article was published, the CLA was a viable option for colleges and universities to determine the relative standing of students in terms of analytic reasoning, problem solving, writing effectiveness, and writing mechanics.[8] A few years later, CAE rolled out a high school adaptation of the CLA, the CWRA.

THE STRUCTURE OF A CAE PERFORMANCE TASK

The CAE's CLA and CWRA performance tasks align with Jay McTighe's seven criteria for performance tasks described in the previous chapter.[9] The CAE tasks

1. require more than recognition or recall; students must use their knowledge and skills;
2. have no single, correct answer due to their open-ended nature;
3. include original, authentic contexts that students find relevant;
4. call for students to thoughtfully apply their knowledge and skills within the contexts;
5. are multilayered and complex; the documents contain different types of information;
6. call for deeper learning proficiencies as well as content-specific knowledge and skills; and
7. yield responses that are scored according to established criteria.

Textbox 4.1 shows one of the first CLA performance task situations. An early rendition of this performance task, titled Crime Reduction, was administered to college students in the study published in 2005. Crime Reduction was retired several years later and used as an exemplar in CAE's Performance Task

Textbox 4.1
SAMPLE CLA PERFORMANCE TASK SITUATION

Pat Stone is running for reelection as the mayor of Jefferson, a city in the state of Columbia. Mayor Stone's opponent in this contest is Dr. Jamie Eager. Dr. Eager is a member of the Jefferson City Council. You are a consultant to Mayor Stone.

Dr. Eager made three arguments during a recent TV interview:

First, Dr. Eager said that Mayor Stone's proposal for reducing crime by increasing the number of police officers is a bad idea. Dr. Eager said "it will only lead to more crime." Dr. Eager supported this argument with a chart that shows that counties with a relatively large number of police officers per resident tend to have more crime than those with fewer officers per resident.

Second, Dr. Eager said "we should take the money that would have gone to hiring more police officers and spend it on the Strive drug treatment program." Dr. Eager supported this argument by referring to a news release by the Washington Institute for Social Research that describes the effectiveness of the Strive drug treatment program. Dr. Eager also said there were other scientific studies that showed the Strive program was effective.

Third, Dr. Eager said that because of the strong correlation between drug use and crime in Jefferson, reducing the number of addicts would lower the city's crime rate. To support this argument, Dr. Eager presented a chart that compared the percentage of drug addicts in a Jefferson ZIP Code area to the number of crimes committed in that area. Dr. Eager based this chart on crime and community data tables that were provided by the Jefferson Police Department.

Mayor Stone has asked you to prepare a memo that analyzes the strengths and limitations of each of Dr. Eager's three main points, including any holes in those arguments. Your memo also should contain your conclusions about each of Dr. Eager's three points, explain the reasons for your conclusions, and justify those conclusions by referring to the specific documents, data, and statements on which your conclusions are based.

Reproduced by permission from the Council for Aid to Education.

Academy, a workshop designed to train educators on the basics of developing performance tasks for their classrooms.

A total of seven documents were created to accompany the Crime Reduction situation. The documents consisted of one page each, and they provided test takers with a wealth of information to synthesize. The following descriptions of the documents were written for this book and were not available to students who took the assessment.

- Document A–Investigator's Memo: A memorandum written by a private investigator who was hired by Mayor Stone to look into possible connections between Dr. Eager and the Strive drug treatment program.
- Document B–Newspaper Story: An article in the local newspaper about a convenience store robbery. The suspect was arrested within hours and appeared to be "high on drugs."
- Document C–Police Tables: Two tables from the Jefferson Police Department showing crime statistics for the city's five zip code areas, the percentage of residents who use illicit drugs, and the percentage of residents who graduated from college.
- Document D–Report on Strive: A research brief from the Washington Institute for Social Research that emphasizes the effectiveness of the Strive drug treatment program in Clarendon, another fictional town.
- Document E–Crime Statistics: A graph from the state Department of Public Safety showing the correlation between robberies/burglaries and the number of police officers per 1,000 residents in the state's fifty-three counties.
- Document F–Dr. Eager's Chart: A chart that Dr. Eager created from the data in Document C, showing the relationship between the number of crimes committed and drug use in Jefferson. Dr. Eager showed the chart during his interview on television.
- Document G–Research Abstracts: Three research abstracts from an online search that used the search terms "drug prevention," "success," and "Strive drug treatment program."

Test takers had ninety minutes to complete a performance task on the CWRA and CLA. For the new CWRA+ and CLA+, test takers have sixty minutes to finish the tasks, which include only one question. The assessments were, and still are, administered online using a split screen, allowing students to type responses in a textbox on one side of the screen while scrolling through the situation and documents on the other side. Textbox 4.2 shows the questions for the Crime Reduction situation, which the students addressed in their mock memos to Mayor Stone.

> **Textbox 4.2**
> **SAMPLE CLA PERFORMANCE TASK QUESTIONS**
>
> 1. Dr. Eager claims that Mayor Stone's proposal "will only lead to more crime" (Document E contains the chart Dr. Eager used to support this claim). What are the strengths and/or limitations of Dr. Eager's position on this matter? Based on the evidence, what conclusion should be drawn about Dr. Eager's claim? Why? What specific information in the documents led you to this conclusion?
> 2. Dr. Eager claims that "we should take the money that would have gone to hiring more police officers and spend it on the Strive drug treatment program." What are the strengths and/or limitations of Dr. Eager's position on this matter? Based on the evidence, what conclusion should be drawn about Dr. Eager's claim? Why? Is there a better solution, and if so, what are its strengths and/or limitations? Be sure to cite the information in the documents as well as any other factors you considered (such as the quality of the research conducted on various drug treatment programs) that led you to this conclusion.
> 3. Dr. Eager claims that "reducing the number of addicts would lower the city's crime rate (Documents C and F exhibit the charts Dr. Eager used to support this statement). What are the strengths and/or limitations of Dr. Eager's position on this matter? Based on the evidence, what conclusion should be drawn about Dr. Eager's claim? Why? What specific information in the documents and any other factors you considered led you to this conclusion?
>
> Reproduced by permission from the Council for Aid to Education.

Saying that Crime Reduction contains a lot of material is an understatement. Other performance tasks on the CLA and CWRA, and now on the CLA+ and CWRA+, are similar in complexity. Each test has a set of several different performance tasks. The tasks are randomly assigned to students when they log in to take the test. CAE described the performance tasks in this manner:

> No two Performance Tasks assess the exact same combination of skills. Some ask students to identify and then compare and contrast the strengths and limitations of alternative hypotheses, points of view, courses of action, etc. To perform these and other tasks, students may have to weigh different types of

evidence, evaluate the credibility of various documents, spot possible bias, and identify questionable or critical assumptions.[10]

A PLAN FOR LOCALLY DEVELOPED TASKS

After we successfully piloted the CWRA at a few high schools, the decision was made to administer the assessment annually to seniors at every VBCPS high school, beginning in 2010. The skills assessed by the CWRA—analytic reasoning and evaluation, problem solving, writing effectiveness, and writing mechanics—were analogous to three of our strategic plan's outcomes for student success. The results of the assessment would track our high school students' progress on critical-thinking, problem-solving, and effective communication skills. Next, we needed an assessment to measure the same skills for elementary and middle school students.

In spring 2009, four VBCPS administrators traveled to CAE headquarters in New York for a two-day Performance Task Academy. During the academy, we reviewed the Crime Reduction task, learned the fundamentals of creating CWRA-type performance tasks, and designed our own performance tasks. One of the tasks invented at the Performance Task Academy, entitled Student Health, was developed further and administered to our fourth graders for eight consecutive years.

Upon returning to Virginia Beach, the associate superintendent for Research, Evaluation, and Assessment assigned two of the administrators who attended the academy to head up a new project. The assignment involved developing performance tasks that mimicked the CWRA but were intended for elementary and middle school students. Additionally, the administrators were responsible for devising workable systems of administering the tasks and scoring students' responses.

The targeted grade levels were fourth and seventh. The main reason for this decision was that fourth- and seventh-grade students were tested fewer times than students in adjacent grade levels. Another reason was that fourth and seventh graders had one year remaining at the same schools, which opened up possibilities for using the results formatively with these students before they moved on to middle or high school.

Because we had an assessment to emulate, we were confident the goals of the project were imminently achievable prior to the following school year. Our first decision was to recruit the best people in the district to help with the work ahead. We asked for recommendations from elementary, middle, and high school principals and from fellow central office administrators. For our team, we were looking for teachers, specialists, and coordinators who had worked previously with performance tasks, as well as teachers who were known as classroom innovators and successful risk takers.

The list we compiled included over forty people with a wide range of pedagogical experience across different grade levels and subjects. The four core content areas were well represented, as were other areas (e.g., family and consumer science, gifted, special education, and technology). In fall 2009, we held an informational meeting for the group. Attendees viewed a presentation that explained the role of performance tasks in our strategic plan, illustrated CWRA performance tasks, and outlined the proposed phases of the project. The first phase, rubric development, was scheduled to begin within weeks after the meeting.

SUMMARY

This chapter told the story of events leading up to VBCPS' decision to assess, en masse, students' deeper learning skills with performance tasks. We started with a strategic plan that emphasized both instruction and assessment of competencies deemed essential for students to succeed in the twenty-first century. Our search for an assessment led us to the CAE's College and Work Readiness Assessment (CWRA). The CWRA performance task became our school district's annual measure of critical thinking and problem solving for high school students and our model for developing performance tasks to administer to younger students.

Here are a few questions for readers who might be considering embarking upon a journey to assess students' higher-order skills on a large scale:

- What is your purpose for assessing deeper learning skills? Do you have an overarching goal, vision, or strategic plan?
- Which skills do you intend to assess? Are the skills defined in your goal, vision, or strategic plan?
- Is there an existing assessment that would serve your purposes? If you plan to develop your own assessment, do you have the necessary personnel and a viable plan?

NOTES

1. William and Flora Hewlett Foundation, "Deeper Learning Defined," April 23, 2013, https://hewlett.org/library/deeper-learning-defined.

2. Los Angeles Unified School District, *A District on the Move: Destination Graduation*, 2016, https://achieve.lausd.net/site/handlers/filedownload.ashx?moduleinstanceid=754&dataid=591&FileName=LAUSD_Strategic%20Plan16-17_vr19F.pdf, 9.

3. Norwalk (OH) City School District, "Mission and Goals of the Norwalk City School District," 2018, http://www.norwalktruckers.net/MissionGoalsoftheNorwalk CitySchoolDistrict.aspx.

4. Virginia Beach City Public Schools, "Compass to 2015: A Strategic Plan for Student Success," October 2008, http://www2.vbschools.com/compass/2015/index.asp.

5. Council for Aid to Education, "What We Do," https://cae.org/about-cae/what-we-do.

6. Stephen P. Klein et al., "An Approach to Measuring Cognitive Outcomes across Higher Education Institutions," *Research in Higher Education* 46, no. 3 (May 2005), 263.

7. Ibid., 268–70.

8. Lee Finkelstein, email to author, July 9, 2018.

9. Jay McTighe, "What Is a Performance Task? (Part 1)," *Performance Task PD with Jay McTighe* (blog), April 10, 2015, *Defined Learning,* https://blog.performancetask.com/what-is-a-performance-task-part-1-9fa0d99ead3b.

10. Council for Aid to Education, *2012–2013 CWRA Institutional Report: Virginia Beach School District*, 19.

Chapter 5

Ruminating on Rubrics

Performance tasks are trending in the field of education, and deservedly so. Well-designed performance tasks engage students in their learning and provide teachers with useful information in ways traditional assessments cannot. On the other hand, there are a number of difficulties associated with performance tasks. Unlike traditional assessments, performance tasks are more challenging to develop, administer, and score than traditional assessments.

As mentioned in chapter 2, scoring was a huge challenge for states during the implementation of large-scale performance assessment programs in the 1990s. No matter what, subjectivity is the proverbial elephant in the room when it comes to scoring performance tasks. Fortunately, there are procedures to shrink the elephant. The initial course of action involves developing effective rubrics.

McTighe's seventh characteristic of performance tasks shown in chapter 3 asserted that "performances on open-ended tasks are evaluated with established criteria and rubrics."[1] This chapter gives a brief overview of rubrics and explains the steps Virginia Beach City Public Schools (VBCPS) undertook to create a rubric for evaluating students' responses to our performance tasks. Chapter 5 is not meant to be an instruction manual for rubric development. Readers seeking detailed information on the construction of rubrics should refer to the sources in the endnotes.

A RAPID RUBRIC REVIEW

In *Understanding by Design*, Wiggins and McTighe stated that a rubric is a "criterion-based scoring guide that enables judges to make reliable judgments about student work and enables students to self-assess."[2] Self-assessment is key to the purpose of rubrics. When a rubric is available to students, they understand the scoring criteria and expectations of the assignment. To allow ongoing self-evaluation, it is best practice for students to have access to the rubric both during the performance and after the task has been completed.

Besides pointing students in the right direction on a performance task, effective rubrics make teachers' jobs easier. In *Creating and Recognizing Quality Rubrics*, Arter and Chappuis stated that rubrics can help teachers

- plan instruction,
- grade consistently,
- provide sound rationale for grades, and
- communicate with parents.[3]

Parents appreciate rubrics because they facilitate better understanding of the often mysterious process of how student work is graded. When teachers or students are going over performance task results with parents, everyone should be looking at the rubric.

Rubrics are either holistic or analytic. Holistic rubrics are used to comprehensively evaluate a performance task product or performance. With a holistic rubric, there is a single, overall score for the product or performance. The main advantage of holistic rubrics is that raters can generate what could be called a quick and dirty score. The main disadvantage is that quick and dirty scores, in many instances, don't yield enough information for students to know why they received the score and how they can improve in the future.

Before discussing analytic rubrics, let's go over the basic structure of a rubric. Susan Brookhart identified a rubric's three parts in her definition: "A rubric is a coherent set of criteria for students' work that includes descriptions of levels of performance quality on the criteria."[4] Figure 5.1 is a good example of an analytic rubric with clearly illustrated parts: levels listed horizontally across the top, criteria listed vertically down the left-hand side, and descriptions in the twelve cells where the levels and criteria intersect.

The rubric in figure 5.1 was created by a former teacher and current education blogger to evaluate the nonacademic task of breakfast in bed. (We recommend it for distribution to spouses and children prior to Mother's Day or Father's Day.) In the rubric there are three essential criteria—food, presentation, and comfort—and four levels: 1. *beginning*, 2. *developing*, 3. *accomplished*, and 4. *advanced*. Each criterion receives a score or rating consistent with the description at one of the levels.

Compared with holistic rubrics, analytic rubrics provide more focused feedback. After students, or breakfast hosts, in the case of figure 5.1, see their scores for their product or performance, they can refer back to the rubric

	Beginning 1	Developing 2	Accomplished 3	Exemplary 4
Food	Most food is colder or warmer than it should be, is under- or over-seasoned, or is under- or overcooked.	Some food is colder or warmer than it should be, is under- or over-seasoned, or is under- or overcooked.	All food is at the correct temperature, adequately seasoned, and cooked to the eater's preference.	All food is perfectly cooked and seasoned to the eater's preference. Additional condiments are offered.
Presentation	More than one item (tray, napkin, or silverware) are dirty or missing.	Tray, napkin or silverware may be dirty or missing.	Food is served on a clean tray, with napkin and silverware. Some decorative additions may be present.	Food is served on a clean tray, with napkin and silverware. Several decorative touches are added.
Comfort	Wake-up is abrupt, little to no help with seating, and the recipient is rushed and crowded during the meal.	Wake-up is somewhat abrupt, recipient may struggle with seat adjustment, or there may be some rushing or crowding during eating.	Recipient is woken gently, assisted in seat adjustment, and given reasonable time and space to eat.	Recipient is woken gently and lovingly, assisted until seating is just right, and given abundant time and space to eat.

Figure 5.1   Breakfast in Bed: Analytic Rubric
Reproduced by permission from Jennifer Gonzalez, "Know Your Terms: Holistic, Analytic, and Single-Point Rubrics," © 2018 Cult of Pedagogy.

and read the descriptors that align with each score. Consequently, they will understand why the scores were awarded and how they can improve their product or performance.

Analytic rubrics are much better than holistic rubrics for formative purposes. Well-written descriptions provide a clear picture of what a product or performance looks like so all stakeholders are able to recognize students' successes and shortcomings on a performance task. At the highest level, exemplary products or performances are described. At the lower levels, the descriptions depict products or performances that are lacking. Creating an analytic rubric usually takes more time than creating a holistic rubric, but it is worth the effort.

LOOKING AT LEVELS

Recall that the top row of cells in the rubric in figure 5.1 are its levels. Levels are also referred to as achievement levels, skill levels, or levels of performance; some experts call them gradations[5] while others use the term *score points*.[6] They can be represented by words, numbers, or both words and numbers, like in the rubric in figure 5.1. The breakfast in bed rubric lists the levels in ascending order from left to right, but levels are commonly arranged in descending order. The rationale behind descending order is to place the highest level of performance adjacent to its respective criterion. In this manner, students will see the description of exemplary first, assuming they read from left to right.

When words or phrases are used to describe levels, rubric developers should take care to choose terms that are appropriate for the targeted student population. Unfamiliar words and negative wording should be avoided. For example, the vocabulary of a typical second grader doesn't necessarily include the word *intermediate*. Because many students—not just second graders—internalize their work, labeling a product or performance as inadequate or ineffective is inappropriate. Such words may lead to hurt feelings and negativity toward a teacher or a task. By the way, *intermediate*, *inadequate*, and *ineffective* were all found on the Internet in age-inappropriate rubrics.

Words used to designate levels should be mutually exclusive. Although rubric creators often believe their level labels are clearly distinguishable, students don't always discern the differences, and overlapping terms may be confusing to the people who use the rubric for scoring. It is questionable whether students or scorers would understand the difference between *good* and *satisfactory* or *amateur* and *acceptable*, pairs assigned to different levels on two other rubrics located on the Internet.

With apologies for using two aforementioned terms, amateur rubric developers frequently inquire about the acceptable number of levels for a rubric. On the low end, many experts advise against two or three levels. There is little justification for developing a two-level rubric. Two-level rubrics merely tell us the product or performance either met or didn't meet the standard for a criterion. A checklist serves the same basic purpose as a two-level rubric.

Well-constructed rubrics with three levels can be successfully implemented; however, there is a downside. The argument for three-level rubrics is that they make it easier for students to understand the differences between low-, medium-, and high-quality responses or products, and they make scoring easier—perhaps a bit too easy. *Regression to the mean* is a statistical phenomenon related to linear regression and the normal curve, topics not addressed in this book. The term has been borrowed and redefined to make the following point about rubrics with three levels.

Similar to rubrics, scorers have different levels of proficiency. Even when scorers are trained adequately, some are immune to training and others always seem to be in a hurry. Rubrics with three levels can result in a type of regression to the mean where regression refers to the deterioration of the scoring process due to scorers regularly awarding scores at the middle level, or mean. Three-level rubrics provide an out for scorers who, for reasons such as indecision and haste, avoid the first and third levels. It should be noted that on any rubric with an odd number of levels, the middle level is a safe place for lazy or ineffective scorers.

On the high end, rubrics with more than six levels tend to complicate scoring beyond what may be necessary. It is hard to come up with reasons to justify a seven-, eight, or nine-level rubric designed for use with a K–12 performance task. While additional training would be required for scorers to distinguish between two adjacent levels in the middle of a rubric with seven or more levels, is there really that much of a difference between a level 5 and a level 6 score?

For the reasons above, our rubric development team, drawn from an array of talented VBCPS educators, decided that four performance levels were just right when we began crafting a rubric to assess open-ended responses garnered from our performance tasks. This was the first time we chose a different path than the developers of the Collegiate Learning Assessment (CLA) and the College and Work Readiness Assessment (CWRA), both scored with six-level rubrics.

We also needed to determine whether we would develop a single rubric or two rubrics—one for each grade level—to evaluate fourth- and seventh-grade responses. We decided to go with a single rubric because ultimately, students from both grade levels would be demonstrating the same critical-thinking, problem-solving, and writing skills on the performance tasks. Although the rubric and structure of the performance tasks were the same for both grades, the degree of sophistication in task content was different for fourth and seventh graders.

The rubric team went back and forth on how to designate each level of our rubric. We believed labeling the levels with words would result in students being labeled as well. Every parent would be proud to know their child wrote an *advanced* response, but not many would be pleased if their child received a *novice* rating. We thought students, teachers, and parents would be more likely to have neutral sentiments about numbers instead of words.

Eventually, we were asked to name the levels so people would know what the numbers meant: Level 1 was termed *novice*; level 2, *emerging*; level 3, *proficient*; and level 4, *advanced*. Level 3 denoted sufficient competence in a skill and level 4 indicated the student had gone above and beyond these expectations. These levels paralleled Arter and McTighe's recommendation for four-level rubrics that "certify competence according to a standard . . . in which '3' is typically defined as the 'standard,' with '4' exceeding the standard."[7]

CONSIDERING CRITERIA

Criteria—also known as performance criteria, evaluative criteria, dimensions, traits, characteristics, or elements—are the learning outcomes, skills, or properties used to judge the product of a performance task. Each criterion is critical to a student's success on the task. The criteria in figure 5.1 appear in the column on the far left of the rubric. Technically, it makes no difference if a rubric has vertical criteria with horizontal levels or vice versa.

When determining how many criteria ought to be included in a rubric, developers should consider all possible criteria that align with the skills or standards the performance task is designed to assess. Then comes the process of selecting the criteria deemed most essential for evaluating the product or performance. Regarding the appropriate number of criteria, iconic assessment authority W. James Popham recommended three to five criteria so as not to overwhelm teachers tasked with scoring.[8]

Like levels, criteria should be mutually exclusive. A rubric for assessing student participation located among countless specimens on the Internet contained the criteria "Level of engagement in class" and "Listening, questioning, and discussing." These criteria seem redundant—aren't listening, questioning, and discussing the most meaningful ways students can engage in class? Redundant criteria can be collapsed into a single criterion. To avoid overlapping criteria, developers should invite constructive criticism and have candid conversations concerning their rubrics with students, colleagues, and other reviewers.

There was plenty of candid conversation when the VBCPS rubric development team met to discuss the criteria for our rubric. We knew the goal was to develop a rubric for scoring student responses for three deeper learning skills, but what we didn't realize at the time—we were undeniably naïve—was the extensiveness of the theory, research, and literature associated with the constructs of critical thinking and problem solving.

Some readers might be familiar with the term *construct*. Briefly, a construct is a theoretical variable that is not directly measurable, such as intelligence or shyness. Constructs are called constructs because they are mentally constructed by humans. Constructs are manifested as observed behaviors or phenomena.[9] To measure a construct indirectly, the behaviors or phenomena linked to the variable must be defined. Constructs like critical thinking and problem solving involve multiple behaviors and multifaceted phenomena, so not all people agree on their definitions. We discovered this when the rubric development team convened for the first time.

The team's long hours of discussion and debate on the aspects and attributes of critical thinking (CT), problem solving (PS), and written communication (WC), will not be revisited here. In short, we got sidetracked from our original goal for at least a day. By executive decree, the conceptual logjam was subsequently broken and the team refocused on rubric development. We decided to narrow, rather than expand, the definitions of CT, PS, and WC to a few observable characteristics that we anticipated would be evident in students' written responses. In other words, we operationally defined our three criteria.

Our first official rubric, shown in figure 5.2, contains our operational definitions of CT, PS, and WC. It is called the IPT rubric because our yet unnamed performance tasks would soon take on the name Integrated Performance task, or IPT. Readers should note that integrated is not the same as interdisciplinary, which means involving two or more subject areas. Whereas interdisciplinary performance tasks purposely incorporate content from different disciplines, our tasks require students to integrate critical-thinking, problem-solving, and writing skills with other skills (e.g., math and citizenship skills).

The original iteration of the rubric included six criteria, or elements: CT1, CT2, CT3, PS, WC1, and WC2. The elements in this rubric corresponded with the original criteria of the CWRA as well as the CLA. The three CT elements on the IPT matched Analytic Reasoning and Evaluation on the CWRA, WC1 was analogous to the CWRA's Writing Mechanics, WC2 was similar to the Writing Effectiveness on the CWRA, and both rubrics had a Problem Solving criterion.

DELVING INTO DESCRIPTIONS

Descriptions, also known as content or descriptors, comprise most of the cells in a rubric. The number of description cells equals the number of criteria times the number of levels. Every cell at the intersection of a criterion and a level contains a description of the performance or product for the specific criterion at the designated performance level. Descriptions at the highest level of performance for each criterion describe what an exceptional performance looks like.

Descriptions in a rubric are all about the quantity and quality of words. Our first piece of advice comes from Popham's article entitled "What's Wrong—and What's Right—with Rubrics." In the article, Popham recognized the widespread popularity of educational rubrics and pointed out a few routine flaws in them. He called one of the flaws *dysfunctional detail*, and based this term on his observation that many rubrics were way too long.[10]

Critical Thinking: Student considers the strengths and weaknesses of the two given options.					
Elements	Level 1	Level 2	Level 3	Level 4
CT1: Identifies and explains important information from the documents provided	Student does not identify any of the important information from the documents, identifies only a small amount of the important information, or explains the information incorrectly.	Student identifies some of the important information from the documents and usually explains the information correctly.	Student identifies a large amount of the important information from the documents and explains the information correctly.	Student identifies all or nearly all of the important information from the documents and correctly explains the information.
CT2: Judges the quality of information in the documents provided	Student does not judge the quality of the information in the documents; the information is repeated and treated as correct and believable by the student.	Student judges the quality of a small amount of the information in the documents and gives reasons why any of the information may be incorrect or hard to believe.	Student judges the quality of some of the information in the documents and gives sensible reasons why any of the information may be incorrect or hard to believe.	Student judges the quality of a large amount of the information in the documents and gives sensible, well-explained, and accurate reasons why any of the information may be incorrect or hard to believe.
CT3: Sees the need for additional information not included in the documents provided	Student does not see the need for any additional information or mentions a need for additional information but does not explain why it is needed.	Student mentions that some additional information is needed and explains why it is needed.	Student gives a satisfactory description of the additional information needed, explains why it is needed, and tells where the additional information could come from.	Student provides a thorough description of the additional information needed, explains why it is needed, tells where the additional information could come from, and explains how the additional information could affect the student's decision.

Problem Solving: Student evaluates information and uses it to defend his/her decision.					
Element	Level 1	Level 2	Level 3	Level 4
PS: Makes a decision and gives reasons for the decision	Student does not make a decision or makes an irrelevant decision; student does not give reasons for the decision, or gives reasons that have nothing to do with the important information in the documents.	Student makes a decision based on some of the relevant information from the documents; the information is usually repeated and may not be explained correctly.	Student makes a decision based on a large amount of the relevant information from the documents and additional information not in the documents; the student's explanation of the information must be correct and sensible.	Student makes a decision based on all or nearly all of the relevant information from the documents and additional information not in the documents; the student's explanation of the information must be accurate, sensible, and persuasive.

Written Communication: Student uses information and ideas to respond in Standard Written English.					
Elements	Level 1	Level 2	Level 3	Level 4
WC1: Demonstrates knowledge of grammar, usage, and mechanics	Student makes frequent errors in grammar, usage, and mechanics; some responses are difficult to read or understand.	Student makes some errors in grammar, usage, and mechanics; errors may hinder understanding in parts of some responses.	Student makes few errors in grammar, usage, and mechanics; errors do not hinder understanding in any responses.	Student demonstrates knowledge of grammar, usage, and mechanics in all responses, which are almost error-free and can be fully understood.
WC2: Presents ideas and information clearly in an organized and detailed manner for the intended audience	Student presents ideas and information that are disorganized and contain few details; sentence structure is not varied and vocabulary is limited; transitions are absent; there is little or no awareness of the intended audience.	Student presents some ideas and information clearly in an organized manner with some details; some variation in sentence structure and vocabulary is present; some responses have transitions; there is some awareness of the intended audience.	Student presents most ideas and information clearly in an organized manner with frequent elaboration; sentence structure and vocabulary are frequently varied; most responses have effective transitions; there is a general awareness of the intended audience.	Student presents almost all ideas and information clearly in an organized manner with consistent elaboration; sentence structure and vocabulary are purposely selected to engage the intended audience; all responses have effective transitions; there is a keen awareness of the intended audience.

Figure 5.2 Original IPT Rubric
Reproduced by permission from VBCPS with use permitted under Creative Commons.

The same problem exists today. A Google search for "critical thinking rubric" yielded some lengthy rubrics, including a six-pager on the website of a well-known educational organization. As mentioned earlier, critical thinking is complicated, so defining its multiple layers concisely in a rubric is a tall order. But a six-page rubric containing approximately 1,800 words in its descriptions is neither practical for teachers who want to determine their students' level of critical thinking nor for students who are attempting to self-assess. Popham endorsed rubrics of one or two pages and warned, "A sheaf of papers held by a staple should be regarded as the enemy."[11]

The best way to limit the size of a rubric is by eliminating unnecessary language in the descriptions. While experts recommend consistent wording, there is a clear difference between consistency and redundancy. For example, all sixteen descriptions in the original IPT rubric in figure 5.2 start with the word *student*. After numerous administrations, we noticed this and eliminated the repetition. The descriptions in later versions of the rubric all begin with verbs.

Repeated language is common in rubrics; it is the consistency component referred to by experts. Descriptions used to define different levels of performance for a criterion will naturally include the same words. This is evident in the rubric in figure 5.2. Three descriptions in the CT2 row start with "Student judges the quality of . . ." The other description begins, "Student does not judge the quality of . . ." Recurrent wording across descriptions is sometimes unavoidable.

Many rubric developers encounter problems with modifiers, especially adjectives and adverbs describing frequency (e.g., *many*, *often*). Just like the terminology used to describe a rubric's levels and criteria, adjectives and adverbs describing frequency should never overlap. It doesn't matter if a rubric developer can perceive subtle differences between modifiers such as *occasionally* and *rarely*. When students or scorers are unable to make the same distinctions between terms as the developer, the instrument needs revision.

Figure 5.2 has several frequency modifiers in the descriptions, including *some* and *most*, a pair seen in the level 2 and 3 descriptions of WC2. The logic behind using these two modifiers in adjacent descriptions might seem obvious but we wanted to rationalize it anyway. Since a large majority of people believe *most* means more than half, it follows that *some* means half or less. Making judgments like this about wording occurs quite frequently while descriptions are being written, so it is best to obtain multiple and varied opinions during the process of rubric creation.

SUMMARY

In the words of Arter and McTighe, "There is no single correct way to develop and use rubrics; however, there are some wrong ways."[12] This chapter provided an overview of rubrics, information about our rubric development experiences, and recommendations for other rubric developers. Here are some key takeaways:

- "The most challenging aspect of designing rubrics for the classroom is in the language used."[13]
- While effective rubrics should contain enough detail for students to self-assess, they should also be as succinct as possible. Finding the right balance is another challenge.
- To maximize rubric improvement, developers should welcome reviews, comments, and suggestions from students, colleagues, devil's advocates, and others.

NOTES

1. Jay McTighe, "What Is a Performance Task? (Part 1)," *Performance Task PD with Jay McTighe* (blog), *Defined Learning*, April 10, 2015, https://blog.performancetask.com/what-is-a-performance-task-part-1-9fa0d99ead3b.

2. Grant Wiggins and Jay McTighe, *Understanding by Design*, 2nd ed. (Alexandria, VA: Association for Supervision and Curriculum Development, 2005), 349.

3. Judith A. Arter and Jan Chappuis, *Creating and Recognizing Quality Rubrics* (Portland, OR: Educational Testing Service, 2006), 31.

4. Susan M. Brookhart, *How to Create and Use Rubrics for Formative Assessment and Grading* (Alexandria, VA: Association for Supervision and Curriculum Development, 2013), 4.

5. Christopher R. Gareis, "Assessment Leadership: Leveraging Performance-Based Assessments for Deeper Learning" (PowerPoint presented at the 2017 School-University Research Network Leadership Conference, Williamsburg, VA, July 20, 2017), https://education.wm.edu/centers/sli/events/learning-leaders-workshop/Gareis%20Leveraging%20PBAs%20for%20Deeper%20Learning%20SURN--July%202017.pdf.

6. Judith Arter and Jay McTighe, *Scoring Rubrics in the Classroom: Using Performance Criteria for Assessing and Improving Student Performance* (Thousand Oaks, CA: Corwin Press, 2001), 29.

7. Ibid., 31.

8. W. James Popham, "What's Wrong—and What's Right—with Rubrics," *Educational Leadership* 55, no. 2 (October 1997), 75.

9. John F. Binning, "Construct," in *Encyclopaedia Britannica*, article published January 22, 2015, https://www.britannica.com/science/construct.

10. Popham, 74.
11. Ibid., 75.
12. Arter and McTighe, 45.
13. Robin Tierney and Marielle Simon, "What's Still Wrong with Rubrics: Focusing on the Consistency of Performance Criteria across Scale Levels," *Practical Assessment, Research & Evaluation* 9, no. 2 (January 2004), 6.

Chapter 6

Developing Performance Tasks

Educators are regularly on the lookout for activities, programs, or practices that have been successfully implemented in someone else's classroom, school, or district. Replication, which is common in education, is not necessarily a bad thing, though renowned educational assessment and policy expert Tom Guskey has reminded us, "Advances in education do not come from imitation; they come from innovation."[1]

Without question, albeit with permission, Virginia Beach City Public Schools (VBCPS) imitated the idea and format of the College and Work Readiness Assessment (CWRA) to develop performance tasks for younger students. The CWRA assesses deeper learning skills for high school students, and our performance tasks were designed to do the same for VBCPS fourth- and seventh-grade students. Before our tasks assumed the name Integrated Performance Task (IPT), a few people referred to them as baby CWRAs.

We never intended to mimic the parent assessment in its entirety. Although much of the IPT project was imitative, it was innovative as well. The VBCPS associate superintendent for Research, Evaluation, and Assessment allowed plenty of leeway for the facilitators—two former elementary and secondary school teachers—to make pragmatic decisions that were in the best interests of the project. We communicated a bottom-up style to the personnel who worked with us on the project, which meant everyone's suggestions were considered.

This chapter gets into the nitty-gritty of developing performance tasks for measuring deeper learning. Near the end of the previous chapter, reference was made to our naïveté at the outset of the project. The information and figures on the following pages illustrate our early, and sometimes misguided, decisions as we surged ahead to create prototypes, conduct field tests, and administer the first IPTs across the district. Our thinking evolved with each experience. An appropriate subtitle for chapter 6 could be "By Seeking and Blundering, We Learn."[2]

WHICH CAME FIRST: THE RUBRIC OR THE TASK?

Developing performance tasks and rubrics for scoring task products is not a linear process—it is iterative. Best practices in assessment and instrument development involve circularity, in which the assessment or instrument is tweaked every time feedback and results warrant improvements. It is an ongoing process of evaluation, revision, and reevaluation. Even though the rubric chapter came prior to the performance task chapter in the book, the best answer to "Which came first, the rubric or the task?" is "They were developed at the same time," which may also be the correct answer to the chicken and egg question.

Jay McTighe, among others, indicated that the first step in rubric development is to obtain samples of student performance that demonstrate the skill(s) targeted by the performance task.[3] Our IPT development team did not follow this advice. Instead, as explained in chapter 5, we skipped ahead and wrote definitions of the characteristics we believed would be evident in student responses to our performance tasks.

Like some professionals are prone to do when tackling a big project, we dove in before fully consulting existing literature or the recommendations of experts. Because we had a draft of a serviceable task created at the Performance Task Academy—Student Health, mentioned in chapter 4—we thought significant progress had already been made. It was not until we field-tested prototypes that we saw how students would react and respond to the tasks, which prompted many changes. It was indeed a circular process.

GETTING A GRASP OF GRASPS

Every CWRA performance task is developed according to a formula. The formula calls for a realistic scenario, or situation, followed by documents and questions intended to engage students and draw out answers that demonstrate critical thinking, problem solving, and writing ability. The situations involve challenging, real-life problems. Students from VBCPS high schools have told us they enjoyed taking the CWRA. There are similar testimonials from students at other schools.[4]

The authentic aspect of the CWRA formula is consistent with a description of performance tasks in *Understanding by Design* (*UbD*), which stated,

"Performance tasks typically present students with a problem: a real-world goal, set within a realistic context of challenges and possibilities."[5] In *UbD*, Wiggins and McTighe introduced GRASPS, a design tool for creating authentic tasks. The acronym stands for "goal," "role," "audience," "situation," "product," and "standards for success." The last "S" was recently amended to "success criteria."[6]

Table 6.1 illustrates the GRASPS elements for our first IPT, Student Health. In every IPT, the *goal* of the student is to make a recommendation based upon given options. Usually, there are only two choices. To keep it simple for fourth graders, the *role* they play is that of a fourth-grade student at a fictitious school, Smith Elementary School. Seventh graders are sometimes given the familiar role of a seventh grader at a made-up middle school, but occasionally they are given another role, such as assistant to a school superintendent.

The *audience* for fourth graders is frequently the principal of Smith Elementary and a principal or superintendent for seventh graders, but each *situation* is different. Making up an IPT situation is considered the fun part, because it requires creativity and collaboration—building upon others' ideas. Many proposed situations don't survive past the brainstorming phase. Other situations grow up to be real live IPTs that are administered across the district.

Returning to GRASPS, the *products* of an IPT are the responses students write to open-ended questions. The *success criteria* are described in the IPT rubric. The authors of *UbD* acknowledged that GRASPS is not meant to be a universal design tool for performance tasks; nonetheless, GRASPS provides an effective framework for developing engaging tasks intended for small- or large-scale administrations.

Table 6.1 GRASPS Elements for Student Health

Element	Representation
Goal	• to recommend a project to improve students' health at Smith Elementary School and support the recommendation with reasons from documents
Role	• a fourth-grade student at Smith Elementary School
Audience	• Mr. Beach, the principal of Smith Elementary School
Situation	• a local business will donate money to the school to pay for only one project—either an outdoor fitness course or a salad bar
Product	• a persuasive letter to Mr. Beach recommending one of the projects
Success criteria	• described in the rubric (see figure 5.2)

Reproduced by permission from Jay McTighe.

PREPARING PROPER PROTOTYPES

To reiterate, assessment development, when done correctly, is a circular process, one which is applicable to teacher-made tests, state-mandated assessments, and everything in between. Revisions based on expert reviews, stakeholder feedback, and test data all contribute to improvement efforts. Although reviews, feedback, and data are readily available, some educators may not know what to do next. The way that educators use the information is often dependent on their degree of assessment literacy.

W. James Popham, in his typical straight-shooting style, once wrote, "What most of today's educators know about education assessment would fit comfortably inside a kindergartner's half-filled milk carton."[7] But Popham wasn't blaming teachers. He pointed out that assessment courses at the undergraduate and graduate levels were "quantitatively intimidating" and mostly irrelevant to the day-to-day circumstances of K–12 schools.[8] In an earlier piece, Popham said this was regrettable, because what "teachers and administrators need to know about testing . . . relies on common sense more than statistical exotica."[9]

We were fortunate to have several assessment-literate educators on our IPT development team. The team also included experienced classroom teachers, which made for an efficient combination of common sense and assessment literacy. The team's job was to assemble two IPT prototypes—one for fourth grade and the other for seventh grade. With summer approaching, we needed to quickly produce both prototypes so there would be time to conduct field tests at schools.

We have always strived for thought-provoking, real-life situations for the IPT. Students are more engaged when instruction is directly connected to their world, and the same is true for assessments. We felt confident that our first attempt at an IPT situation, Student Health, would interest fourth graders. The situation involves a local business that wants to donate money to Smith Elementary School to improve students' health. The money must be used to pay for either an outdoor fitness course or a salad bar.

We believed our seventh-grade situation would trigger a strong reaction among young adolescents, since it was based on a recent controversy at a local shopping mall. The issue, which still exists at the same mall and other malls across the United States,[10] involves a chaperone policy that restricts unaccompanied minors' access to the mythical Beach Mall. The test taker's role is a teenager serving on a committee formed by mall officials. The teen's goal is to write a recommendation to the mall officials concerning the policy. We predicted (correctly) that many responses would be fervent, emotional rants against the policy, so students were instructed to support their recommendation with evidence from the documents provided with the situation.

Several documents offered the evidence students needed to incorporate in their responses to attain a *proficient* or *advanced* score. Some documents contained information that was meant to distract or mislead—so-called red herrings—while information in other documents was more or less neutral. The documents in the grade 7 Mall Chaperone IPT were

- a flyer promoting the "family-friendly" Beach Mall;
- a somewhat biased news story;
- a graph of crime statistics in the area adjacent to the mall;
- a social media site complete with comments; and
- a research brief citing recent studies on youth violence.

The documents in the grade 4 Student Health IPT were

- a fact sheet outlining children's playground injuries;
- a news story describing the benefits of salad bars; and
- an advertising brochure exalting outdoor fitness courses.

Both IPTs culminated with a series of questions intended to extract answers that would allow us to see what students perceived as the pros and cons of the choices. Before finalizing the prototypes for field-testing, we asked several VBCPS staff members to review everything we had written. Our reviewers were veteran teachers and administrators from various schools and departments, including personnel from the Office of Programs for Exceptional Students and the Department of Research, Evaluation, and Assessment. Because most of them had no prior involvement with the IPT project, this group of reviewers provided us with feedback from a fresh perspective.

FINE-TUNING WITH FIELD-TESTING

As noted earlier, the IPT development team had a tight deadline for completing performance tasks to administer in the fall to every fourth- and seventh-grade student. Marc Chun, the former director of education at the Council for Aid to Education (CAE), summarized the timeline for developing performance tasks for the Collegiate Learning Assessment (CLA), the forerunner of the CWRA, as follows:

> Creating performance tasks as standardized assessment tools requires a high level of expertise and the investment of significant time and resources. A team of measurement scientists spends 18 months building each of the performance tasks used as part of the CLA. These tasks must meet the highest standards of

reliability and validity, and the process includes numerous rounds of field-testing, revision, and calibration.[11]

With the first large-scale administrations planned for October, our timeline was about half the time allotted for developing a CWRA or CLA performance task. We needed to field-test as soon as possible.

Field-testing was arranged with elementary and middle school principals who were willing to allow prototypes to be administered at their schools for the greater good of the district. Besides having enough students for the field tests, we needed the right teachers to help us. The cooperating principals astutely selected teachers who were enthusiastic about playing a part in the development of a new type of assessment. The contagious effect of teacher enthusiasm was also a boost. Before, during, and after the field tests, the students cooperated beyond our expectations.

Dozens of field tests have been conducted since 2010, but the procedures are essentially the same. First, the facilitator—not the teacher—explains to the students that

- their class was specially chosen to take a new assessment;
- their scores on the field test will not count as a grade; and
- the purpose of the field test is to try out this new assessment so it can be improved for other students.

Sighs of relief are audible once students learn the field test will not affect their academic standing. Every now and then, a student asks, "Are we the guinea pigs?" The answer is an unequivocal yes. Fourth-grade students are also told they might actually enjoy the experience, and many do. We don't use the same approach with seventh-grade students, who are sometimes more cynical than their younger counterparts. Older students are simply informed that their teachers will receive the results of the field test so they can better understand how the students think and solve problems.

We always consider the possibility of a Hawthorne Effect, especially at the elementary level. Research buffs may recall that the Hawthorne Effect "refers to the effects of subjects' awareness of their evaluation as participants of a research study."[12] The fourth graders in our field-testing groups are told that their principal chose them specifically for a special project. There's no doubt the performance of some students—even at the middle school level—is better on the field tests than it might be for a regular administration, but that is fine with us. We need to see what responses from motivated students look like.

Not only are we interested in seeing how the most motivated and brightest students respond, we want to read typical responses from other students as well. Field tests are conducted at elementary and middle schools across Virginia Beach. We ask principals at almost every school to designate nongifted classes for field tests. These procedures generate responses and reactions as diverse as the student population in our district.

After asking students to do their best when answering the questions, we invite them to provide written feedback during the field test. Students are told to circle words and phrases that a typical fourth or seventh grader may not be able to read or understand. We never say, "Circle words or phrases *you* aren't able to read or understand," because students might be less likely to circle a word or phrase, preferring not to disclose their perceived academic shortcomings.

On occasion, students offer candid, comprehensive critiques. Some critiques contain a crumb that could potentially diminish the IPT's authenticity in the eyes of other students. For example, the grade 7 IPT always includes a mock social media page and students are quick to point out anything they think is amiss on the page, such as the true meaning of an emoji. Elementary and middle school students often perceive an IPT's content and design differently than adults do. We believe the best advice about tests frequently comes from the test takers themselves. It's no wonder teachers appreciate the old adages "out of the mouths of babes" and "kids say the darnedest things."

An informal focus group commences as soon as the field-test responses have been collected, giving students another chance to add their two cents' worth. The first question we ask is whether the situation is something that could have really happened. We've never been told a situation is contrived, nor have we heard remarks like "This is stupid" or "Who would ever do that?"[13] Even the staunchest young critics usually admit the situation could probably occur.

Next, we ask our focus group about ways in which the IPT could be improved. Students suggest clearer, more genuine vocabulary and recommend minor revisions to the format. Most of the suggestions have merit and many are incorporated in later versions of the IPT. Focus groups typically wind down with the facilitator fielding questions from the students. The students' questions indicate their overall curiosity about assessing deeper learning skills and testing in general. These discussions have proven to be a rich opportunity to engage students in conversations about how and why they are assessed, dialogue which, unfortunately, does not occur as often as it should.

We prefer employing fourth- and seventh-grade classes for field-testing, but sometimes we are unable to try out a new performance task on the targeted grade level. When a new IPT is developed in the middle of the school year for an end-of-year administration, we recruit fifth- or eighth-grade classes, thus avoiding a preview of the task for fourth- or seventh-grade students and teachers. Fifth- and eighth-grade guinea pigs have worked well, due in part to their familiarity with a type of test they took earlier in their school careers.

Field-testing is an essential undertaking in the assessment development process. Despite having full plates and tight deadlines, educators at the school and district levels should always find time to field-test new assessments. This fairly simple procedure can do much to prevent problems with an assessment as well as concerns about the validity of its results. In sum, field-testing can help educators ascertain whether a test is assessing what it was intended to assess.

INITIATING INAUGURAL ADMINISTRATIONS

While expert feedback, field tests, and focus groups all yield invaluable information for improving a performance task, there is nothing like a large-scale administration to reveal unforeseen issues. Approximately 10,000 fourth- and seventh-grade students took the first IPTs in fall 2010. People who have overseen district or statewide test administrations realize the rarity of everything going off without a hitch. Various things did go wrong during the debut of the IPT. Saying the rollout was an eye-opener would be grossly understating the experience.

With a mixture of confidence and uncertainty, we launched the IPT across the district. Memos, instructions, and administration guidelines preceded the arrival of IPT packets at VBCPS elementary and middle schools. Principals were informed that all fourth- and seventh-grade students would take the IPT during a three-week window, with teachers then scoring each student's responses.

There was a lot of shock and pushback when teachers learned the news. Many saw the IPT as just another test the central office was unloading on them. Very few knew anything about the assessment, so rumors abounded. At times, we thought our maiden voyage would end abruptly, but the superintendent and his district leaders stood fast. Every elementary and middle school dutifully complied—the IPT era was under way.

The plan was for students to read the IPT packets and type their answers on computers. The responses would be saved on Schoolnet, the online assessment platform used by our district. Each student needed a laptop or desktop computer with Internet access for approximately two hours: thirty minutes to log in and receive instructions plus ninety minutes to finish the task.

Figure 6.1 shows the first page of Student Health, the first IPT administered districtwide to fourth-grade students. One of our best decisions was having fourth-grade teachers read the entire packet aloud to their classes before

Developing Performance Tasks 65

 Children's Health

Doctors agree that the two most important ways for children to stay healthy are by being active and eating the right foods. Children who eat right and get exercise usually get sick less and live longer than children who eat mostly junk food and spend most of their free time on the computer, watching TV, or playing video games.

Situation

You are a 4th-grade student at Smith Elementary School. A local business has given your school a large sum of money to help students be healthier. The money must be used to pay for only one of these projects:
- An outdoor fitness course at the school
- A salad bar for the school cafeteria

Some students want a salad bar and some students want a fitness course, but the school cannot have both. Your principal, Mr. Beach, has asked you to help him choose the project that will be better for promoting student health at Smith Elementary School.

Mr. Beach wants you to read some information before you answer his questions. He expects you to think about the information and pick the project that will be better for promoting student health at Smith Elementary School.

Salad Bar

Fitness Course

Figure 6.1 Grade 4 IPT Situation—Fall 2010
Reproduced by permission from VBCPS with use permitted under Creative Commons.

students were allowed to begin typing answers. Unless a test's specific purpose is to evaluate students' reading comprehension, efforts should be made to ensure that reading ability does not affect the results.

Unlike fourth-grade teachers, seventh-grade teachers did not read the entire IPT. The middle school version was much longer than the elementary IPT, so teachers read only the directions and situation out loud to their classes. Teachers at both levels were also instructed to "read any word, phrase, or sentence in any document aloud to students who ask for help." Unfortunately, some students don't request help for fear of being stigmatized.

Student responses are the product of every IPT. The answers to questions are used to score students' critical-thinking, problem-solving, and written communication skills, so the wording of questions is vital. We call the questions on the IPT "prompts," because they are not all in the form of a question. There were five prompts on the initial IPTs. Here are the fall 2010 grade 4 prompts:

1. Describe any information that was not in the documents that could help you make a wise choice between the salad bar and the fitness course for promoting student health at Smith Elementary School. Tell where the other information would come from and explain how this information could help you decide which project is better for promoting student health at Smith Elementary School.
2. What did you think about the information that was in the documents (fact sheet, news story, and brochure)? Did any of the information seem incorrect, hard to believe, incomplete, or misleading? If you said yes, describe this information.
3. What are the strengths and weaknesses of the salad bar? Use information from the documents to explain your answer.
4. What are the strengths and weaknesses of the fitness course? Use information from the documents to explain your answer.
5. Which project is better for promoting health for the students at Smith Elementary School? Explain the reasons you made this choice.

The grade 7 IPT also contained five prompts similar to the grade 4 prompts, except that they were related to the mall chaperone policy. The last prompt was more complicated for seventh-grade students. The middle schoolers were told, "Write a recommendation to the mall's management about whether or not to continue the mall chaperone policy. Considering both of the issues of (1) safety and security for the mall's customers and (2) profits for all of the mall's stores, provide a detailed explanation describing why you made this recommendation."

ENHANCING AND ADVANCING

After persevering through our initial districtwide administrations, we made an analogy between the development processes of an IPT and a new medication. Even though a pharmaceutical company tests and retests a new drug before it is approved for public distribution by the US Food and Drug Administration (FDA), it is not until the public has used the medication that the company and FDA discover all of its flaws. Table 6.2 illustrates the full analogy.

Developing Performance Tasks 67

Table 6.2 Comparison of drug development and IPT development processes

Drug Development Process	IPT Development Process
Step 1—Discovery and development	→ Brainstorming and prototype production
Step 2—Preclinical research	→ Expert reviews and revisions
Step 3—Clinical research	→ Field-testing and additional revisions
Step 4—FDA review	→ Final review
Step 5—FDA postmarket safety monitoring	→ Districtwide administration

U.S. Food and Drug Administration, "The Drug Development Process," last updated January 4, 2018, https://www.fda.gov/forpatients/approvals/drugs.

FAIRNESS AND ALIGNMENT

The remainder of this chapter focuses on two critical topics in the development of any performance task. Ensuring that the task is fair for all students and aligned with its rubric should be of utmost concern to any developer, yet these things are often ignored. The IPT evolved into an operative large-scale assessment because we took on difficult issues like these and came up with practical solutions.

Fundamental Fairness

According to the *Standards for Educational and Psychological Testing*, "fairness is a fundamental validity issue and requires attention throughout all stages of test development and use."[14] Recall from chapter 3 that validity addresses whether a test assesses what it is supposed to assess. Fairness, and the related term *bias*, have to do with "the extent in which a test score . . . [is] valid for all intended individuals and groups."[15] That is, fair assessments yield results that aren't biased for or against any students.

Two fairness issues were brought to our attention shortly after the inaugural administration of the grade 4 IPT, Student Health. An assistant principal of a school in a low-income neighborhood informed us that there were fourth graders in her school who had no idea what a salad bar was. In addition, teachers at other schools pointed out that many children hate salad. Naturally, these students chose the fitness course over the salad bar. The Student Health IPT was biased against salad haters and students who, for reasons beyond their control, didn't eat at restaurants with salad bars. The evidence in the Student Health documents was supposed to steer students toward the salad bar. Playground accidents are the leading cause of injury to children ages five to fourteen, and salad bars—which can be used year-round—are more inclusive than outdoor fitness courses.

We decided that fixing Student Health was a better option than throwing out the task. First, we asked several fourth-grade teachers to find out whether students who disliked salad would eat fruit, cheese, or vegetables, food commonly available at many salad bars. The results of the straw poll indicated almost every student would eat fruit, cheese, or both. It came as no surprise that vegetables were not very popular.

Next, we prepared PowerPoint presentations for fourth-grade teachers to show their classes before the next administration of Student Health. The presentation's primary purpose was to explain the IPT rubric and how the students' responses would be scored for critical thinking (CT), problem solving (PS), and written communication (WC). It also included slides picturing outdoor fitness courses and fruit and salad bars, along with narration describing what they are. The revised IPT may still have been unfair to a small number of students, though our actions helped level the playing field.

For the spring administrations, the IPT development team fashioned new situations for both grade levels. Like the initial IPTs, we thought our new situations and documents were relevant and plausible. Additionally, the spring IPTs were printed in booklet form, not the stapled packets of their predecessors, which presented problems when students removed the staples from their packets.

Another fairness issue came to light while the spring IPT responses were being scored. The new situation once again took place at the fictional Smith Elementary School, where Principal Beach was troubled by bad behavior during lunch. The task was titled Lunchroom Behavior, and the solutions were hiring two extra lunchroom monitors or reducing the time permitted for lunch from thirty to twenty minutes. Using documents based on factual information about best practices for school cafeterias and the amount of time students should be allotted for lunch, we attempted to steer students toward the choice of hiring extra monitors.

Steering test takers via information in documents is a tactic employed in CWRA and CLA performance tasks, although it is unlikely CAE employees will ever admit a task has a *right* answer. For performance tasks at the high school and college levels, subtle clues often appear in graphs, tables, or detailed documents. For fourth- and seventh-grade students, the evidence is in plain sight. A CLA or CWRA response can attain a high score by endorsing any of the given choices, but only if the response includes a cogent argument. An IPT response that ignores the obvious will not reach the *proficient* level in PS.

The Lunchroom Behavior fairness problem emerged after hundreds of responses had been scored. Fourth graders were generally falling in line with the notion that hiring more lunch monitors was Mr. Beach's best option. Students were unwilling to accept that more instructional time due to shorter lunches was the better choice. But students at one school were adamant that a shorter lunch period was the way to go. This school had a policy of rewarding classes who demonstrated exemplary behavior during the first part of lunch, and well-behaved classes were allowed to go outside for recess after they finished eating. The majority of fourth graders at this school disregarded the evidence in the documents, assumed shorter lunches meant there would be recess, and declared that twenty minutes for lunch was best.

Instead of revising the Lunchroom Behavior IPT, we abandoned it and returned to the drawing board for the following spring's grade 4 task. Other IPTs have been discarded for reasons besides fairness. For example, we recently disposed of a grade 7 performance task because it was not challenging enough. The documents included blatant rationale to support one choice and lacked reasons of substance for the second choice, so the recommendation was a no-brainer. Consequently, the PS scores for this IPT were the highest ever recorded for a seventh-grade cohort.

Educators who do not explore the possibility of bias on an assessment are negligent. If a test contains anything that would unfairly affect the results for one or more groups, action needs to be taken. Sophisticated statistical techniques for detecting test bias exist, but educators can avoid certain fairness issues simply by using common sense and having their assessments scrutinized by various people, including students.

Essential Alignment

About the same time that teachers began scoring responses from the initial districtwide administrations, we realized the IPT needed serious changes prior to the next testing window. Many elementary and middle school principals invited the facilitators who headed up the project to conduct on-site training sessions with their staff. The sessions opened with discussions about the IPT's origin and purposes. Then we trained teachers to use the rubric for scoring students' responses. The next chapter addresses the training of teachers in greater detail.

Teachers were quite inquisitive at the training sessions, but we sensed a degree of angst and skepticism, especially among teachers whose students had recently taken the IPT. The sessions afforded opportunities for frank conversations with teachers, which allowed us to gain valuable insights that were otherwise unattainable. One such insight resulted in a fundamental change that kept the IPT project afloat for years to come.

At the training sessions, we presented these scoring instructions to staff:

- Read one student's responses to all five prompts.
- Responses to a single prompt should not be scored in isolation.
- The rubric elements do not correlate independently with corresponding prompts.

Looking back, we had been thinking too large when we developed the rubric and initial IPTs. We were guilty of overlooking the realities of classroom teachers' everyday jobs. Would teachers really have the time to read multiple responses from each student and award six separate scores according to six different rubric criteria?

It was fitting that a suggestion from an unassuming teacher caused an epiphany. The suggestion was simply, "Why don't you match each prompt with a rubric element?" The name of the teacher, her school, and the answer to her question are long forgotten, but the idea sparked conversations that resulted in new prompts, a revised rubric, and more practical ways for teachers to score responses. These improvements transformed the IPT into a functional districtwide performance task.

Our changes to the rubric and prompts occurred simultaneously. We decreased the number of rubric elements and prompts, then matched each prompt with an element. The first order of business was eliminating CT1, "Identifies and explains important information from the documents provided." There was no need for students to do this because the information would—or would not, depending on the depth of the response—be identified and explained when they wrote about their choice. We aligned the other CT elements with the first two prompts and matched PS with the third and final prompt. Prompt 1 responses would be scored exclusively for CT1, prompt 2 responses would be scored only for CT2, and prompt 3 responses would be scored for PS.

The last order of business was reducing WC to a single rubric element. We eliminated WC1, "Demonstrates knowledge of grammar, usage, and mechanics." In doing so we once again parted ways with the CWRA, which included writing mechanics as a criterion in its rubric. While using standard written English is a skill high school students must master in preparation for college and work—the "C" and "W" in CWRA—we concluded that overemphasizing grammar and spelling on the IPT would be a mistake. Our reasoning follows.

At some point in their careers, many, perhaps most, teachers have been asked, "Does spelling count?" When students are told misspellings will count against them, they tend to limit their compositions to words they know how to spell, rather than using their full spoken vocabulary. We wanted students

Developing Performance Tasks 71

to express their ideas on the IPT without having to worry about perfection in spelling, grammar, or punctuation. How students thought and solved problems was of much greater importance. That's not to say we completely discounted poor spelling or bad grammar. Responses that were difficult to read or understand would likely receive low scores across the board.

The responses to prompt 3 at both grade levels were the students' recommendations to a predetermined audience (e.g., Principal Beach, mall officials). We decided that, in addition to scoring for PS, prompt 3 responses would be scored for WC. This simplified the scoring process because teachers could look at a single response—instead of all three—to rate the writing effectiveness of a student. After a little wordsmithing, we introduced a revised IPT rubric in spring 2011 (see figure 6.2).

Figure 6.3 shows the three prompts we used when Student Health was administered again during the following year. Similar prompts for different situations were included in every spring and fall IPT for the next several years. The last document in both the fourth- and seventh-grade booklets contained the "incorrect, unbelievable, or misleading" information alluded to in prompt

INTEGRATED PERFORMANCE TASK (IPT) RUBRIC

Critical Thinking: Student analyzes the information to determine its relevance, quality, and depth.

Elements	Level 4	Level 3	Level 2	Level 1
CT1: Judges the quality of information in the IPT documents	Student judges the quality of a large amount of the information in the documents and gives sensible, well-explained, and accurate reasons why any of the information may be incorrect or hard to believe.	Student judges the quality of some of the information in the documents and gives sensible reasons why any of the information may be incorrect or hard to believe.	Student judges the quality of a small amount of the information in the documents and gives reasons why any of the information may be incorrect or hard to believe.	Student does not judge the quality of the information in the documents. Student treats the information as correct and believable.
CT2: Sees the need for information not included in the IPT documents	Student gives a detailed description of other information needed, explains why it is needed, and explains how the other information could affect the student's decision.	Student gives a satisfactory description of other information needed and an appropriate explanation of why it is needed.	Student gives a basic description of other information needed and a basic explanation of why it is needed.	Student does not see the need for any other information or states that other information is needed but does not provide any explanations.

Problem Solving: Student evaluates the information and uses it to defend his/her decision.

Element	Level 4	Level 3	Level 2	Level 1
PS: Makes a decision and gives reasons for the decision based on information from the IPT documents and other information not in the documents	Student makes a decision based on many relevant reasons from the documents and other information not in the documents. The reasons must be explained fully and correctly and the explanation must be sensible and persuasive.	Student makes a decision based on some relevant reasons from the documents and at least one other reason not in the documents. The reasons must be explained fully and correctly and the explanation must make sense.	Student makes a decision based on a small number of relevant reasons from the documents. The reasons may not be explained fully and correctly.	Student makes a decision but does not give any relevant reasons from the documents for the decision, student does not make a decision, or student makes an irrelevant decision.

Written Communication: Student uses information and ideas to create a clear, organized response.

Element	Level 4	Level 3	Level 2	Level 1
WC: Presents information and ideas that are clear, organized, detailed, and written for the intended audience	Student presents almost all of the information clearly. The information is organized and has: • advanced vocabulary, • consistent detail, • frequent variation in sentence structure, • effective transitions, and • consistent awareness of the intended audience.	Student presents most of the information clearly. The information is organized and has: • above basic vocabulary, • frequent detail, • some variation in sentence structure, • appropriate transitions, and • consistent awareness of the intended audience.	Student presents some of the information clearly. The information is organized and has: • basic vocabulary, • some detail, • little variation in sentence structure, • some transitions, and • some awareness of the intended audience.	Student presents information that is unclear or disorganized and has: • limited vocabulary, • little or no detail, • no variation in sentence structure, • no transitions, and • little or no awareness of the intended audience.

Figure 6.2   2011 IPT Rubric
Reproduced by permission from VBCPS with use permitted under Creative Commons.

1. The advertisement on page 5 (Document 3 - "Fitness 4 Kids Outdoor Fitness Courses") gives information that tells why schools need an outdoor fitness course.
   - Review the advertisement and find all of the information that you think may be incorrect, unbelievable, or misleading.
   - Give reasons that explain why you thought the information was incorrect, unbelievable, or misleading.

2. Sometimes we need more evidence or information to help us make a wise choice. Describe any information that was **not** in the booklet or **not clearly explained** that would help you decide which project would be better for promoting health for all of the students at Smith Elementary School.
   - Describe the information you would need that was **not** in the booklet or **not** clearly explained in the booklet.
   - Explain why you need this information.
   - Explain how this information could help you make a wise choice.

3. Write a persuasive letter to Mr. Beach explaining your choice for promoting health for all students at Smith Elementary School. You **must** choose **only one** of these two projects: an outdoor fitness course **or** a fruit and salad bar. You may use information from your answers to Prompts 1 and 2 to help you write your letter.

   You should include all of the following in your letter:
   - ☐ A greeting (Dear Mr. Beach,)
   - ☐ An opening sentence that tells which project you are recommending to Mr. Beach
   - ☐ Reasons from the booklet and reasons that were not in the booklet that support your recommendation
   - ☐ A final sentence that summarizes your recommendation
   - ☐ A closing (Yours truly, A Fourth-Grade Student)

   Do **not** type your name on the letter.

   greeting → Dear Mr. Beach,
   closing → Yours truly,
   A Fourth-Grade Student

Figure 6.3   Fall 2011 Grade 4 IPT Prompts
Reproduced by permission from VBCPS with use permitted under Creative Commons.

1. This document was placed on the page adjacent to prompt 1 so students could easily refer to it while answering the prompt.

SUMMARY

This chapter covered the development and implementation of the IPT. Producing viable tasks is an iterative process that involves reviewing, revising, field-testing, more revising, and administrating on a large scale, which results in further revisions. Field-testing established how long an administration would take, what kind of vocabulary was appropriate, and whether students found our situations and documents to be credible. Marc Chun likened the development of performance tasks to playwriting: "If we think of performance tasks, like theater, as constantly evolving, we realize that the key is to listen to students like a playwright listens to an audience and to constantly improve."[16]

The initial IPTs included five open-ended prompts. Responses were scored according to six criteria. After the first districtwide administrations, we learned that asking students to answer—and teachers to score—responses to five prompts was just plain oppressive. The next iteration had three prompts and a rubric with four criteria. By listening to the people who administered, took, and scored our performance tasks, we made sensible changes that made it easier to administer, take, and score the IPT.

A number of takeaways from chapter 6 are listed below. The suggestions are not limited to developing districtwide performance tasks; most are germane to the development of different types of assessments for classrooms, districts, and states.

- If feasible, find an existing assessment (e.g., CWRA) or a framework (e.g., GRASPS) that suits the purposes of the assessment you plan to develop. There's no need to conform to every detail of the model while developing the new assessment.
- Invite constructive criticism from colleagues and other professionals during the development process.
- Field test the assessment with a diverse group of students. Debrief with the students after field testing.
- Revise as needed. If warranted, field test a second time with a different group of students. Revise again pending the group's feedback.
- Administer the assessment on a full scale. Debrief with the teachers who administered it.
- Make more revisions after the first full-scale administration as well as after subsequent administrations if the revisions will improve the assessment.

NOTES

1. Thomas R. Guskey (@tguskey), "After responding today to nearly 20 requests for names of schools that 'are already doing it,' this may bear repeating. Our approach too often is: 'Before doing what strong evidence shows is better for kids, I'd like to talk to others who have already done it just to be sure,'" Twitter, January 22, 2018, 11:48 a.m., https://twitter.com/tguskey/status/955527650977701888.

2. Johann Wolfgang von Goethe, quoted in James Wood, *Dictionary of Quotations from Ancient and Modern English and Foreign Sources* (New York: F. Warne and Company, 1899), 34, https://www.bartleby.com/345/9.html.

3. Judith Arter and Jay McTighe, *Scoring Rubrics in the Classroom: Using Performance Criteria for Assessing and Improving Student Performance* (Thousand Oaks, CA: Corwin Press, 2001), 37; Grant Wiggins and Jay McTighe, *Understanding by Design,* 2nd ed. (Alexandria, VA: Association for Supervision and Curriculum Development, 2005), 181.

4. Tony Wagner, *The Global Achievement Gap: Why Even Our Best Schools Don't Teach the New Survival Skills Our Children Need—and What We Can Do About It* (New York: Basic Books, 2008), 117; "St. Gregory Students Discuss College and Work Readiness Assessment (CWRA) Test," video, 4:41, April 1, 2010, https://www.youtube.com/watch?v=w20K0YY22IA.

5. Grant Wiggins and Jay McTighe, 157.

6. Jay McTighe email message to author, May 8, 2018.

7. W. James Popham, "All about Accountability—Needed: A Dose of Assessment Literacy," *Educational Leadership* 63, no. 6 (March 2006), 84.

8. Ibid.

9. W. James Popham, "All about Accountability—Why Assessment Illiteracy Is Professional Suicide," *Educational Leadership* 62, no. 1 (September 2004), 83.

10. "Youth Supervision Policy," MacArthur Center, 2018, https://www.shopmacarthur.com/youth-supervision-policy; "Parental Escort Policy," Mall of America, 2018, https://www.mallofamerica.com/security/parental-escort-policy.

11. Marc Chun, "Taking Teaching to (Performance) Task: Linking Pedagogical and Assessment Practices," *Change: The Magazine of Higher Learning* 42, no. 2 (March/April 2010), 24.

12. Renee L. Allen and Andrew S. Davis, "Hawthorne Effect," in *Encyclopedia of Child Behavior and Development*, ed. Sam Goldstein and Jack A. Naglieri (Boston: Springer, 2011), https://link.springer.com/referenceworkentry/10.1007%2F978-0-387-79061-9_1324.

13. Grant Wiggins and Jay McTighe, *Solving 25 Problems in Unit Design: How Do I Refine My Units to Enhance Student Learning?* (Alexandria, VA: Association for Supervision and Curriculum Development, 2015), 26.

14. American Educational Research Association, American Psychological Association, and National Council for Measurement in Education, *Standards for Educational and Psychological Testing* (Washington, DC: American Educational Research Association, 2014), 49.

15. Lloyd Bond, Pamela Moss, and Peggy Carr, "Fairness in Large-Scale Performance Assessment," in *Technical Issues in Large-Scale Performance Assessment*, ed. Gary Phillips (Washington, DC: National Center for Education Statistics, 1996), 119.

16. Chun, 27.

Chapter 7
Scoring Performance Tasks

Within six months of the initial rollout of the Integrated Performance Task (IPT), an efficient system of administering performance tasks to thousands of students across our school district had been fine-tuned. Devising a viable method to score the tens of thousands of responses written by these students would take much longer. Although scoring performance task products at the district level involves many of the same challenges as scoring at the classroom level, large-scale scoring endeavors are far more complicated than small-scale efforts. Planning for districtwide scoring, especially in a sizable district like Virginia Beach City Public Schools (VBCPS), is onerous, detail-oriented work, with unanticipated issues constantly arising.

The current chapter examines how time and resources were utilized to score the multitude of IPT responses generated by VBCPS students twice annually. The main topics in this chapter are interrater agreement, centralized and decentralized scoring, and computer scoring. Readers who plan to score performance task responses on a large scale should heed our mistakes and how we corrected them. Readers should also note that the terms *rater* and *scorer*, as well as *ratings* and *scores*, are used interchangeably throughout the chapter.

INTERRATER RELIABILITY AND INTERRATER AGREEMENT

Maximizing objectivity is one of the greatest challenges of scoring performance task products. In a truly objective scoring operation, the same products will consistently receive the same ratings by different people who independently score the same products. This is usually called *interrater reliability*; however, we use the term *interrater agreement* because the concept is unlike other types of reliability. Traditional types of reliability—equivalence, internal consistency, and stability—appear as statistical estimates based on data from tests and test items, while interrater reliability (i.e., interrater agreement) is "a specific instance of reliability where inconsistencies are not attributed to differences in test forms, test items, or administration occasions, but to the scoring process itself, where humans, or in some cases computers, contribute as raters."[1]

Interrater agreement is heavily affected by rubric quality and rater training, and so is its lesser known cousin, *intrarater agreement*. Intrarater agreement is the degree that an individual rater has scored consistently, irrespective of when and under what conditions the rater was scoring. A high level of intrarater and interrater agreement is needed for performance task results to be considered valid for their intended purposes. Both are affected by internal factors such as fatigue and mood, and external factors such as noise and time constraints.

DECENTRALIZED SCORING ACROSS THE DISTRICT

The difference between decentralized scoring and centralized scoring is fairly simple. For the IPT, decentralized meant each school's responses were scored at the schools. Centralized scoring refers to scoring the entire district's responses at a single location. There are advantages and disadvantages associated with both methods. This section recounts our experiences with on-site, decentralized scoring.

As mentioned in the previous chapter, several principals invited the IPT project facilitators to their schools to conduct scorer training with their faculty. Other than teachers who scored IPT field-test responses, it's doubtful that any VBCPS elementary or middle school teachers had ever scored students' responses specifically for critical thinking and problem solving. As we headed out to the schools, we were again venturing into largely uncharted, and this time, possibly dangerous waters. Unlike the field-test scorers, most of the teachers who attended the training sessions were not there voluntarily.

At some schools, we worked with a library or lunchroom full of people. Principals at these schools wanted to expose their entire faculty—including art, music, physical education, and other special area teachers—to scoring with rubrics. At other schools, principals decided that training one or two teachers at each grade level was sufficient. In the same way that lower pupil to teacher ratios are better for students, lower scorer to facilitator ratios resulted in better training sessions.

A few principals saw the IPT as strictly a fourth- and seventh-grade initiative and assigned all scoring duties to their fourth- or seventh-grade teachers. The following year, a memo went out to elementary and middle school principals reiterating our strategic plan's emphasis on "teaching and assessing those skills our students need to thrive as twenty-first-century learners, workers, and citizens."[2] Promoting critical thinking, problem solving, and effective communication was a districtwide initiative and principals were encouraged to employ more than just fourth- and seventh-grade teachers for decentralized scoring.

At the beginning of the training sessions, we handed out copies of multipage scoring guides to the trainees. The scoring guides were expanded versions of the IPT rubric, mostly bullet-pointed scoring instructions and sample responses for each rubric criterion at different levels. The IPT rubric—often referred to as the student rubric—was created as a general rubric applicable to every IPT. Scoring guides—we called them teacher rubrics—were task-specific rubrics written to score responses for each unique version of the IPT. The multipage teacher rubrics were much more detailed than the student rubrics and were intended to make it easier for teachers to score students' responses.

Susan Brookhart pointed out that task-specific rubrics serve as scoring directions for raters because "they detail the elements [i.e., characteristics] to look for in a student's answer to a particular task."[3] Using a task-specific rubric, raters are not required to make as many inferences compared to scoring with a general rubric. This means there will be less subjectivity, higher interrater agreement, and shorter training sessions with task-specific rubrics. Due to their specificity, this type of rubric is essentially an answer key and should not be shared with students in advance.

After teachers received their scoring guides, they were shown a PowerPoint presentation. The presentations ranged from twenty-seven slides for after-school training sessions to seventy-seven slides for extended sessions held on teacher workdays. The bulk of slides in the PowerPoints focused on the six IPT rubric criteria and the application of the criteria to sample responses. Numerous samples of actual student responses were included in the presentation. These responses were copied and pasted onto slides, and the words, phrases, and sentences that provided insight into how the responses were scored were underlined.

At the end of each session, the teachers scored several responses independently. This was followed by calibration, an activity vital to training any group of scorers—even groups as small as two. To calibrate means "to check, adjust, or determine by comparison with a standard."[4] This definition describes the purpose of calibration for scoring performance task responses.

During calibration, trainees compare ratings and discuss the reasons they scored the way they did, one response at a time.

The rubric should be the foundation of every discussion in the calibration process. Statements such as "This is a 4 because I think this student writes well" or "It just looks like it should be a 1" are unacceptable rationale for awarding a score. Justifying a score must be based on general rubric criteria or task-specific rubric guidelines. The *standard* mentioned in the definition of *calibrate* in the preceding paragraph is the standard set by the rubric, not the group's standard. In other words, a group of trainees shouldn't tweak anything in the rubric, even if they disagree with it.

Responses used for calibrating new raters should be vetted and scored ahead of time by persons with in-depth knowledge of the rubric and scoring guide. If unscreened or unscored responses are used for calibration, the trainees—led by one or more outspoken people—might attempt to hijack the training session. Regardless, every logical argument for or against a given score should be heard. After a prescored response is discussed within a calibration group, the expert's score should be shared and explained (e.g., "This response *is* a 4 because . . ."). While it is possible some trainees will contest the score, most will likely assent.

Rubrics that are appropriately developed, reviewed, and tried out before being rolled out usually pass muster with a group of new raters. Using a rubric that has not been appropriately vetted may turn the training session into a dispute about what the rubric ought to include. The purpose of calibration is not to critique the rubric but to give raters ample opportunities to check and adjust their thinking so that it is fully aligned with the rubric. This is known as internalizing the rubric.

Our training sessions varied from school to school in terms of the number of trainees, the interest levels of trainees, and the time allowed for training. These variables affected the accuracy of ratings and interrater agreement between scorers. The approaches taken by elementary schools in scoring dozens or, at middle schools, hundreds of students' responses also influenced accuracy. At some schools, responses were distributed evenly among trained teachers and were each scored once. At other schools, responses were scored by two or three teachers. Building-level decisions dictated the approaches to scoring.

Despite our training efforts, we were certain that interrater agreement for decentralized scoring was low. Schools were not expected to submit their scores—they were intended exclusively for school use—but through anecdotal evidence and spot checks, we saw inconsistent ratings within schools and between schools. Besides insufficient training, there was another major factor that led to scoring imprecision: the nature of the teaching profession.

Teachers who attend to all aspects of the job, as many readers probably know, are continually busy. They frequently work more than forty hours per week with no overtime pay. Scoring performance task responses was seen by some teachers as just one more thing that was forced upon them. Based on our knowledge of teachers' workloads and how they prioritize work, we thought it was unlikely that *every* teacher took the time to read *every* response carefully and consult the scoring guide before awarding *every* score.

Although decentralized scoring had plenty of shortcomings, it was an endeavor that taught us valuable lessons. After the number of criteria on the IPT rubric was reduced to four and the number of prompts was cut to three, training sessions became easier from the perspective of trainers and trainees alike. Decentralized scoring shaped our ideas about ways to decrease subjectivity and increase interrater agreement as we moved on to the challenges of centralized scoring.

ADVENTURES WITH CENTRALIZED SCORING

Presentations to students and faculty, memos to principals, and letters to parents conveyed the message that the IPT was a low-stakes test. Unlike high-stakes tests, whose purposes include using results "to make important decisions about students, educators, schools, or districts,"[5] IPT scores had no significant consequences for VBCPS students, teachers, or schools. The presentations, memos, and letters also communicated the different purposes of the fall and spring IPTs.

In the fall, the purpose of the IPT was to introduce students to a new type of assessment. Results were intended strictly for formative use. Spring results were used as key indicators for the Compass to 2105 strategic plan at the school and division levels. Since the spring IPT was a summative assessment with scores shared publicly, we needed a tighter, more accurate system of scoring spring responses. Centralized scoring was the obvious answer.

Unquestionably, we learned more from our initial centralized scoring effort than from any other endeavor described in this book. We made some intelligent decisions, but other parts of our plan bordered on disaster. While much time and money were wasted in the initial effort, the experience ultimately led to an efficient and cost-effective process for scoring hundreds of thousands of responses over the next five years.

We began by recruiting prospective scorers. Every VBCPS elementary and middle school principal received a memo asking them to nominate teachers who were willing to score IPT responses during the upcoming summer break. The pay rate was $25 per hour, more than double the starting hourly rate that

Pearson offers to scorers.[6] Our plan was to have each response rated independently by two teachers. If the pair's ratings did not match, a third scorer broke the deadlock. The final list of nominees included approximately 200 names. Nearly all elementary and middle schools in the district—plus a few high schools—were represented.

Our first mistake was failing to screen scorers. After several scorers were not paid for the first pay period, we found out that their teaching contracts had not been renewed for the following school year. The payment issue was promptly rectified, but the attitude of some of the nonreturning teachers was not. In general, they were less committed to the work than the contracted teachers were. From then on, we hired only people who had VBCPS teaching contracts for the fall.

Concerning scheduling, we made good, fair, and poor decisions. The IPT scoring cadre, as we called it, met for five hours per day, four days per week, until every response was scored. We knew after field-testing that scoring hundreds of open-ended responses could be mentally exhausting for an individual. Typically, teachers can fully engage in scoring for two to three hours at a stretch provided they are well rested and motivated. Even the most stalwart scorer's concentration begins to dissipate at some point, which affects interrater and intrarater agreement.

Our daily scoring schedule for the cadre called for two and one-half hours of scoring in the morning, followed by a thirty-minute lunch period. Scoring resumed after lunch for another two and one-half hours. Paid breaks were planned for the morning and afternoon, though not every scorer took advantage of them. Sometimes a scorer would plow through lunch and the breaks, scoring paper after paper without respite. While we appreciated the dedication of our scorers, this appeared to be unhealthy. Hourly stretching breaks and half-hour lunches became mandatory for all future scoring cadres.

Another mistake was related to the scheduling of training sessions and workweeks. We correctly assumed a full day was necessary to transform teachers into effective IPT scorers. The mistake resulted from our decision that teachers needed to work only a minimum of one four-day week. Some cadre members served as scorers for one week and others scored for multiple weeks, but not necessarily consecutive weeks. New scorers were trained every Monday and then scored for the rest of the week. On the cadre's second week, both new scorers and returning scorers showed up for work. It was the same for the third and fourth weeks.

During the third week we noticed a surge in the number of responses being routed to third scorers, which meant more and more ratings from the first two scorers did not match. We investigated the problem and saw substantial discrepancies between the ratings of new scorers and the ratings of returning scorers on the same responses. The level of interrater agreement between inexperienced scorers and experienced scorers was unacceptable.

The revolving door method of training and scoring was the main cause of this problem. At the same time new scorers were just getting the hang of it, other scorers were already adept at the job. On occasion, different people conducted training sessions, so somewhat dissimilar interpretations of the rubric and scoring guide were communicated to trainees. The quick fix for the interrater agreement issue was immediate retraining for the entire scoring cadre. We also had to go back and rescore numerous responses. The scoring assembly line was temporarily halted and, as they say, time is money.

To keep this situation from recurring, we established new hiring and scheduling policies for successive years. To be considered for an IPT scorer position, a teacher had to come to work every day for at least the first two weeks. The only training sessions were held on the first day of the very first week. This requirement reduced our scorer pool to less than 150, but interrater agreement received a boost due to uniform training. Scorers were trained by the same people and became more proficient at the job because they worked consecutive weeks.

For the second year of the scoring cadre, we expanded upon an idea put into practice during our first centralized scoring effort. From the start, we knew scoring students' responses for written communication (WC) was inherently different than scoring responses for critical thinking (CT) and problem solving (PS). The people who scored WC—mostly top-notch elementary and secondary English language arts teachers—evaluated the overall quality of students' writing, while those who scored CT and PS responses were tasked with finding indicators of critical-thinking and problem-solving ability, as specified by the rubric and scoring guides.

Scoring only one element worked out well for our WC scorers, but the scorers who scored both CT and PS struggled somewhat when they needed to shift mindsets to score responses for the two different rubric elements. The following summer, we divided our scorers, already split by elementary and middle school, into separate groups to be trained on a lone IPT element. The idea was to turn each teacher into a scoring specialist for a single element.

During the first year, neither personnel nor data were managed well. Although the IPT project facilitators thought everything was pretty well organized in advance, we didn't anticipate that every inquiry or concern, no matter how trivial, would end up coming to us. Scoring performance tasks was brand new to nearly everyone we hired, and because most of them wanted to do well on the job, they had a lot of questions.

At times, we felt we were under siege; responses needed to be printed and copied, papers had to be distributed, scored papers piled up, scorers sought permission to come in late or leave early, and so forth. Consequently, we gave battlefield promotions to a few deserving teachers. Our trusted lieutenants, who quickly learned the ropes, disseminated and retrieved response papers, entered data on spreadsheets, and answered many of the scorers' questions.

For the second summer of scoring, we designated a room leader and an assistant room leader for each of the eight scoring rooms. It was really a quasipromotion—room leaders and assistant leaders were paid the same hourly rate as scorers. The difference was that leaders had additional responsibilities that gave them more hours than scorers. Besides training and managing scorers, the leaders' responsibilities included distributing and retrieving response papers and timesheets, recording scores, and serving as third scorers. The rank-and-file scorers never resented their room leaders. In fact, they seemed to prefer being supervised by responsible peers.

Data management was by far the biggest blunder of our first summer scoring adventure. A coherent procedure for distributing papers and tracking responses was lacking. Due to frequent miscommunication, previously scored responses were often rescored for no apparent reason. The most glaring goof involved a response that received separate ratings of level 1, level 2, level 3, and level 4 on PS from four different scorers! When a baseball player hits a single, double, triple, and home run in the same game, it is called hitting for the cycle. When we saw that the same IPT response was scored at all four levels, it was like hitting a brick wall. With improved organization and consistent training in subsequent years, this error was merely a one-hit wonder.

Thanks to the room leader system that was instituted in year two, data and personnel issues were largely resolved. To further strengthen our staff structure during succeeding summers, we enlisted two of our best room leaders to oversee the scoring cadre at each grade level. For want of a better name, we called the two teachers "lead room leaders." These people, as well as almost all of our room leaders and scorers, were consummate professionals that any principal would be proud to hire.

The lead room leaders were given increased responsibilities; they managed the other leaders, the glut of paperwork, and data for the rooms in their charge. For this they were granted a modest raise of five dollars per hour. We relied heavily on our lead room leaders. They saw the big picture and contributed mightily to the success of centralized scoring. They also helped compile interrater agreement statistics, something we began calculating after the first year's fiasco.

Calculating interrater agreement is fairly simple. It is the percentage of responses that receive the exact same score from two different scorers. By determining interrater agreement data for individual scorers, we found out which scorers would need to be retrained. Not coincidentally, the room leaders already knew who these people were. We never shared interrater agreement stats below the room leader level because we aspired to have a collegial rather than a competitive work environment.

As soon as the IPT scoring cadre was finished for the summer, interrater agreement stats were calculated for each scoring room. Interrater agreement percentages for rooms ranged from 66 to 82 percent over the years. Again, it came as no surprise to room leaders and lead room leaders when a room's percentage fell below 70 percent, which is analogous to the interrater reliability statistic .70 considered acceptable by many testing experts.[7]

There were two main reasons why some rooms obtained lower interrater agreement percentages than others. Calibration—actually the absence of it—was the first reason for low interrater agreement. Each morning, room leaders led calibration activities using prescored responses. Sometimes there was not enough calibrating. While several room leaders stopped to calibrate every two hours or so, other room leaders did it only once a day.

The second reason was the difficulty of scoring some responses versus scoring other responses. Even with extensive training, calibration, and use of detailed scoring guides, many responses to a particular prompt on certain IPTs were downright hard to score. In his exposé of how big testing companies score open-ended responses, Todd Farley put it like this: "The best of rubrics are always just trumped by the deluge of student responses they are written to assess."[8]

Except for the first year, centralized scoring was quite an accomplishment. Up to 40,000 scores were finalized annually during the four- to five-week periods. To obtain the scores, every response was scored twice, sometimes three times. Responses to prompt 3 were scored separately for PS and WC, so they were reviewed four, five, or six times. In all, our scoring cadres of fewer than 150 teachers amassed 100,000 discrete scores per year, give or take a few thousand.

PROS AND CONS OF MACHINE SCORING

Not long ago, Linda Darling-Hammond wrote, "Technological advances are beginning to enable highly reliable computer-based scoring of complex student responses."[9] As an alternative to human IPT scoring—a system that had been in place for five years—VBCPS looked at the possibility of machine scoring, also known as automated essay scoring. A request for proposals was sent out, a company named Turnitin was awarded the contract, machine scoring was successfully piloted, and the Turnitin Scoring Engine became the sole method of scoring IPT responses in Virginia Beach.

The rationale behind the decision can be summed up in three words: ease, speed, and cost. The plan was for teachers, who were no longer required to score fall IPT responses, to use the additional time to review students' prescored responses. Furthermore, the Turnitin Scoring Engine meant fourth- and seventh-grade teachers could review their students' responses and scores from the spring IPT before the end of the school year, instead of waiting until the following fall. As soon as the scoring engine was trained, results were returned posthaste.

The clincher was cost. Like most technology, automated scoring has become more sophisticated and affordable in the twenty-first century. Needless to say, the decision was unpopular with scoring cadre teachers, many of whom had worked with us for four or five consecutive summers. Yet the decision was understandable. Organizations adopt machine scoring due to "funding shortages and probably, in some cases, [they] need lower-cost alternatives to continued levels of funding."[10]

Training a machine to score requires human scorers. Every time a new IPT is administered to students, a few of our most experienced scorers rate a large sample of responses, which are then fed into the Turnitin Scoring Engine. Human scorers who rate with consistency produce scored responses that allow the engine to do the same as it creates and then utilizes countless algorithms. In essence, automated scoring systems replicate the scoring patterns garnered from the hundreds of prescored responses that are used to train them.

Statistically, scoring IPT responses by machine has been comparable to human scoring. Reliability estimates have ranged from .64 to .85 for the Turnitin Scoring Engine, paralleling the scoring cadre's interrater agreement range of 66 to 82 percent. The engine has regularly attained values of .70 or higher, considered the benchmark for low-stakes assessments scored by machine.[11] In addition to being cheaper, easier, and faster than its human counterparts, the scoring engine appeared to score just as well as our scoring cadre had in the past.

Table 7.1 compares the strengths of human raters with those of automated essay scoring systems. Despite automated scoring being more precise, objective, and consistent, it is performed by a machine that is unable to comprehend the meaning of text. A number of educators and educational organizations are opposed to automated essay scoring, particularly for high-stakes tests.[12] The objections are, in part, related to the items in the first column of table 7.1—the qualities of good writing that humans are able to judge but machines cannot, such as creativity and critical thinking.

The Turnitin Scoring Engine delivers numerical ratings on students' responses to IPT prompts, but it does not offer feedback. Before machine scoring entered the conversation, the IPT scoring cadre put in place a procedure

Table 7.1 Measurement strengths of human raters and automated essays scoring

Human raters are able to incorporate as part of a holistic judgment:	Automated systems are able to more efficiently provide:
• artistic/ironic/rhetorical styles • audience awareness • content relevance (in depth) • creativity • critical thinking • logic and argument quality • factual correctness of content and claims	• granularity (evaluate essays with detailed specifications with precision) • objectivity (evaluate essays without being influenced by emotions and/or perceptions) • consistency (apply exactly the same grading criteria to all submissions) • reproducibility (an essay would receive exactly the same score over time and across occasions)

From Mo Zhang, "Contrasting Automated and Human Scoring of Essays," *Educational Testing Service: R&D Connections*, no. 21, March 2013. Reproduced by permission from the Educational Testing Service.

for providing feedback, along with scores, to students and teachers. When a rating at the *novice* or *emerging* level was awarded, scorers checked off one or more predetermined reasons why a response received the rating. Examples of reasons were "No clear choice given" and "Questionable and/or unclear reasoning." The feedback, though not detailed, gave students and teachers a place to start when discussing ways to move students toward proficiency.

Having teachers keep an eye out for disturbing responses was another standard procedure of the IPT scoring cadre. Every summer, scorers brought to our attention several responses containing sentences or paragraphs that mentioned bullying or school violence on a personal level rather than in the context of the IPT situation. We matched the response with its writer and alerted the principal of the student's school with an email that included the passage and the student's identity. Even when a scoring engine is programmed to track specific words and phrases, it isn't as efficient as teachers in identifying disconcerting information. Acting in the best interests of children is what teachers do.

Meanwhile, the debate about the better method for scoring open-ended responses on a large scale continues. If financially feasible, the best way is to use both humans and machines, a method employed by many large testing companies. Hybrid scoring is used to score performance task responses for the Collegiate Learning Assessment and the College and Work Readiness Assessment, and the model aligns with the thinking of some assessment authorities, who believe that machine scoring "should be construed primarily as a *complement* to (instead of replacement for) human scoring, *limited* in its ability to measure a subset of the writing construct."[13]

SUMMARY

Scoring open-ended responses, especially on a large scale, is arguably the most challenging undertaking associated with a performance task program. Unlike test items on traditional assessments, performance tasks typically do not have a single correct answer, which means subjectivity always comes into play. Although state-of-the-art machine scoring is undeniably a triumph of modern technology, it is not a silver bullet. Human judgment is required to train automated scoring systems, and machines are unable to recognize certain features of deeper learning.

Regardless of the scale of the scoring enterprise, recommended best practices include

- extensive training of scorers on the correct use and interpretation of the rubric;
- open discussions about rubric interpretation to get scorers on the same page;
- ongoing calibration with diverse samples of responses; and
- retraining and further calibration whenever it is necessary.

If these practices are implemented appropriately, the inevitable subjectivity of scoring performance task responses can be greatly reduced.

NOTES

1. Tony Albano, *Introduction to Educational and Psychological Measurement: Using R* (Self-published, GitHub, 2018), https://www.thetaminusb.com/intro-measurement-r/reliability.html#interrater-reliability.

2. Virginia Beach City Public Schools, *Compass to 2015: A Strategic Plan for Student Success*, October 2008, http://www2.vbschools.com/compass/2015/index.asp.

3. Susan M. Brookhart, *How to Create and Use Rubrics for Formative Assessment and Grading* (Alexandria, VA: ASCD, 2013), 10.

4. *American Heritage Dictionary of the English Language,* 5th ed. (Boston: Houghton Mifflin, 2011), 264.

5. *Glossary of Education Reform*, s.v. "High-Stakes Test," last updated August 8, 2014, https://www.edglossary.org/high-stakes-testing.

6. Valerie Strauss, "Congratulations to Me. I Have Been Offered a Position as a Professional Scorer by Pearson," *Answer Sheet* (blog), *Washington Post,* April 14, 2015, https://www.washingtonpost.com/news/answer-sheet/wp/2015/04/14/congratulations-to-me-i-have-been-offered-a-position-as-a-professional-scorer-by-pearson.

7. Anna Lind Pantzare, "Interrater Reliability in Large-Scale Assessments: Can Teachers Score National Tests Reliably without External Controls?" *Practical As-*

sessment, Research & Evaluation 20, no. 9 (April 2015), 6, https://pareonline.net/getvn.asp?v=20&n=9.

8. Todd Farley, *Making the Grades: My Misadventures in the Standardized Testing Industry* (Sausilito, CA: PoliPoint Press, 2009), 199.

9. Linda Darling-Hammond, *Developing and Measuring Higher Order Skills: Models for State Performance Assessment Systems* (Washington, DC: Council of Chief State School Officers and Learning Policy Institute, February 2017), 45.

10. Ken S. McAllister and Edward M. White, "Interested Complicities: The Dialectic of Computer-Assisted Writing Assessment," in *Machine Scoring of Student Essays: Truth and Consequences,* ed. Patricia Freitag Ericsson and Richard H. Haswell (Logan, UT: Utah State University Press, 2006), 25.

11. David M. Williamson, Xiaoming Xi, and F. Jay Breyer, "A Framework for Evaluation and Use of Automated Scoring," *Educational Measurement: Issues and Practice* 31, no. 1 (Spring 2012), 7.

12. See, for example, Peter Greene, "Automated Essay Scoring Remains an Empty Dream Human," *Education* (blog), *Forbes,* July 2, 2018, https://www.forbes.com/sites/petergreene/2018/07/02/automated-essay-scoring-remains-an-empty-dream/#18cdaa2974b9; Human Readers, *Professionals against Machine Scoring of Student Essays in High-Stakes Assessment,* 2013, http://humanreaders.org/petition/research_findings.htm; and National Council of Teachers of English, *NCTE Position Statement on Machine Scoring: Machine Scoring Fails the Test,* April 20, 2013, http://www2.ncte.org/statement/machine_scoring.

13. Yigal Attali, "Validity and Reliability of Automated Essay Scoring," in *Handbook of Automated Essay Evaluation: Current Applications and New Directions,* ed. Mark D. Shermis and Jill Burstein (New York: Routledge, 2013), 182.

Chapter 8

Using Performance Task Results

While psychometricians—experts in the science of mental measurement—are primarily concerned with applied theory and techniques of test development and scoring, and testing personnel attend mostly to administrating tests and reporting results, educators are mainly interested in the ways that test results can be used to improve teaching and learning. This chapter focuses on the formative and summative uses of Integrated Performance Task (IPT) results by Virginia Beach City Public Schools (VBCPS) teachers and administrators.

Chapter 8 is divided into two sections. The first section examines the reliability and validity of IPT results, and the second section discusses how the results have been used at the classroom, school, and district levels. A few statistical concepts and psychometric terms appear in the first section, though efforts have been made to avoid hypertechnical explanations. The methods we employed to address reliability and validity include best practices in the development of assessments for large-scale administration. Some of these procedures can be used by teachers as they create assessments for their students.

IMPORTANCE OF RELIABILITY AND VALIDITY

Assessment literate educators recognize the importance of reliability and validity, yet many large-scale assessments—including tests administered at the district level—go unchecked for reliability and have little or no evidence of validity. This section explains why reliability and validity are vital, and it recounts the ways we determined that IPT results were reliable and valid for their intended purposes.

The *Standards for Educational and Psychological Testing* defined reliability as "the degree to which test scores for a group of test takers are consistent over repeated applications of a measurement procedure and hence are inferred to be dependable and consistent for an individual test taker."[1] So why should educators care about reliability? Scores from unreliable assessments—tests that measure inconsistently or erratically—can lead to inaccurate conclusions and inappropriate instruction for individuals or groups of students.

Reliability estimates range from 0 (no reliability) to 1.0 (perfect reliability). For performance tasks, test reliability involves the degree to which different administrations of the same task yield relatively stable results over time. To ascertain the reliability of IPT scores in terms of their stability, we analyzed school-level data for a grade 7 task, School Hours, administered at every VBCPS middle school over two consecutive years. The reliability for the critical thinking (CT) scores of School Hours was .96, problem solving (PS) and written communication (WC) were each .98, and the overall reliability for the task's scores was .99. We couldn't have asked for better numbers. (The School Hours task is included in appendix B.)

Most methods of determining reliability aren't practical for use with teacher-made assessments;[2] however, validity is another matter. Why should educators care about validity? To answer a question with another question, who wouldn't want to know if the inferences drawn from a test's results are defensible? Validity is "the overarching concept that defines quality in educational measurement."[3] A test itself cannot be valid or invalid. Validity refers to the interpretation of a test's results and the way the results are used.

Sometimes we hear about an assessment having face validity. Popham described face validity as verisimilitude, or "having the appearance of truth."[4] Another scholar suggested that face validity is mainly about public relations.[5] Many people see face validity as simply an assumption as to whether a test *appears* to assess what it was intended to assess. We could have reported that the IPT's face validity was adequate and left it at that, but we opted to pursue credible evidence of validity.

Content validity, also known as content-related evidence of validity, concerns the relationship between a test's content and the construct the test was designed to measure.[6] Examples of constructs commonly measured at schools are spelling aptitude and algebraic thinking. On a multiple-choice test, each item should align with a specific learning objective. On a performance task, the content should be relevant to, and representative of, the domain of the construct(s) the task is supposed to measure.[7] For the purposes of the IPT, we wanted to know if each task's content was appropriate for eliciting students' responses that would allow valid inferences about their proficiency in critical thinking, problem solving, and writing.

Evidence of content validity is typically obtained through what are called expert judgments.[8] Although Mark Twain said that "an expert is an ordinary fellow from another town,"[9] we recommend using qualified experts. Legitimate experts—people whose judgments provide credible evidence—are learned authorities in a field directly connected to the content of the test, for example, a mathematician for a math test or a fluent French speaker for a French test.

Our experts included veteran VBCPS educators, described in chapters 4 and 6. Their collective knowledge of teaching and assessing fourth- and seventh-grade students was invaluable. Every detail of the IPT was scrutinized during the initial development phase. Since we wanted more than judgments from our own people, we brought in a fellow from another town. This was no ordinary fellow. At the time, Marc Chun was director of education at the Council for Aid to Education and is widely regarded as the brains behind Collegiate Learning Assessment (CLA) and College and Work Readiness Assessment (CWRA) performance tasks. He now works at the William and Flora Hewlett Foundation. Marc carefully examined our rubric and IPTs, suggested several changes, and put his stamp of approval on our first two tasks.

In general, content-related evidence of validity is sufficient for teacher-made tests. Teachers, as experts, should have the necessary judgment to determine whether their tests are instructionally valid, meaning they are aligned with what students are being taught.[10] Likewise, performance tasks created for classroom usage "need not adhere to . . . rigorous psychometric standards."[11] Conversely, assessments developed for administration on a large-scale or for high-stakes purposes (e.g., graduation, program placement) should have evidence beyond content validity to support claims that they measure what they were intended to measure.

We sought additional evidence of validity for the IPT by conducting a criterion validation study. Criterion-related evidence of validity is acquired by correlating the scores of one test administration with the scores of a different test administered to the same examinees. The second test, known as the criterion, should be an assessment with existing evidence of validity for measuring the construct the first test is supposed to measure. The strength of the correlation between the scores of the first test and the criterion indicate the degree to which the tests are measuring a common construct. A correlation that is sufficiently strong provides criterion-related evidence of validity for the first test.[12]

Because finding the perfect criterion is often problematic, we followed this advice: "There must be judicious tradeoff in selecting a criterion which (1) can be reliably measured within the time and cost constraints of the study and (2) will have a relationship to the ultimate criterion of interest to most test takers."[13] As our criterion test, we chose the California Critical Thinking Skills

Test (CCTST), a series of age-appropriate assessments designed to measure "the core reasoning skills needed for reflective decision making concerning what to believe or what to do."[14] The CCTST uses real-life scenarios with challenging problems and answer options presented in a multiple-choice format. The tests have ample evidence of reliability and validity.

During a one-week testing window, VBCPS students at thirteen schools were administered the elementary or middle school versions of the spring IPT and CCTST. This was a purposeful sample. In other words, we selected the samples because they were collectively representative of the district's grade 4 and 7 populations with respect to ethnicity and gender.[15] The number of students in each group exceeded the minimum sample size of 200 recommended by some researchers.[16] Table 8.1 shows the correlations, also known as validity coefficients, which resulted from our criterion validation study. Validity coefficients range from +1.0 to −1.0.

There is no universal agreement concerning an acceptable value for validity coefficients. When asked, "What is a good validity coefficient?" the legendary educational psychologist Lee Cronbach said it was "the best you can get."[17] Cronbach explained that correlations as low as .20 can still be good enough for the test in question to "make an appreciable practical contribution" for understanding the meaning of scores.[18]

As shown in table 8.1, the correlations between IPT scores and overall CCTST scores ranged from .29 to .42, indicating that the two assessments measured, to a moderate degree, the same construct. Constructs exist only in a theoretical sense, so it is open to debate whether the construct could be called critical thinking, problem solving, or something else. Nevertheless, the statistically significant validity coefficients between the scores of the two assessments—both purported to measure critical thinking—served as evidence that the IPT measured at least one, and perhaps other deeper learning skills.[19]

SUMMATIVE AND FORMATIVE USES OF IPT RESULTS

Just as it is incorrect to say that an assessment is valid or not valid, labeling an assessment as summative or formative is erroneous as well. An assessment, in and of itself, cannot be summative or formative. Summative and forma-

Table 8.1   Correlations between IPT scores and CCTST scores

Group	Number of Students	CT1	CT2	PS	WC
Grade 4	207	.36	.29	.33	.35
Grade 7	395	.37	.41	.31	.42

tive refer to how the results of an assessment are actually used. This section explains how VBCPS educators have used IPT results for summative and formative purposes.

Using IPT Results at the District Level

As discussed in chapter 4, the IPT was originally envisioned as a means of summatively assessing progress on the VBCPS strategic plan. After each spring's IPT responses were scored, the percentages of students with scores at level 2 or higher (i.e., *emerging*, *proficient*, or *advanced*) for CT, PS, and WC were calculated for the district. Fourth- and seventh-grade percentages were computed separately and reported as annual VBCPS Key Academic Measures.

Three years after the IPT was introduced, we realized that comparing the percentages from year to year could sometimes lead to faulty conclusions about our students' growth, or lack of growth, on the skills measured by the assessment. The problem stemmed from administering different performance tasks in successive years or administering a task that had undergone major revisions from one year to the next. In either case, the relative difficulty levels of various IPTs had been overlooked, so valid comparisons of the results could not be made.

Textbox 8.1 shows a portion of a brief report written to point out the problem. The term *task equivalency*, as used in the report, refers only to the level of difficulty for different IPTs at the same grade level. Task equivalency is not as technical as the term *alternate forms*, which means that different versions of an assessment are interchangeable due to "the same content and statistical specifications."[20]

The equivalency problem was partially resolved by administering identical IPTs in consecutive years. Questions arose again after there were serious discrepancies between the overall scores of two fourth-grade cohorts who took the same version of the task in back-to-back years. The inconsistency in scores was explained by differences in scoring. Between administrations of this particular IPT, the scoring method was changed from human rater to scoring engine. Despite the machine's satisfactory levels of agreement with human-scored responses, the machine awarded lower ratings, on average, than the ratings given during the prior year by the IPT scoring cadre.

Year-to-year comparisons using IPT results, or the results of any test, should be made with caution. Even if the two test forms are of equal difficulty, differences between the characteristics of groups of test takers can affect the results. Other variables that influence test scores include test preparation, testing conditions, and adherence to standardized administration

> **Textbox 8.1**
> **THE CASE FOR INTEGRATED**
> **PERFORMANCE TASK EQUIVALENCY**
>
> The results of numerous assessments are used as Key Academic Measures for the Virginia Beach City Public Schools (VBCPS) Compass to 2015 strategic plan. Comparisons are made so progress on the outcomes for student success can be evaluated annually for VBCPS and each school. For the comparisons to be valid, it is essential that the measures from which the results are obtained are the same from year to year. Because measures such as Advanced Placement Exams and the ACT College Readiness Benchmarks rarely undergo major revisions, valid comparisons can be made between the results of these key academic measures for similar samples of students over the years.
>
> Included among the key academic measures are scores from the Integrated Performance Task (IPT), which provide an indication of students' proficiency in the areas of Critical Thinking 1 (CT1), Critical Thinking 2 (CT2), Problem Solving (PS), and Written Communication (WC) in grades 4 and 7. During spring 2012 and 2013, two different IPT scenarios at each of these grade levels were presented to students. While the intent of the IPT development teams was to create performance tasks that were similar with regards to difficulty level—and field tests suggested that the new IPTs were comparable to previous IPTs—this was an assumption that could not be confirmed until large-scale administrations of the new IPTs had taken place and the students' responses were scored.

procedures. When test taker, test prep, or test-taking practices differ from administration to administration, fair comparisons between scores are tenuous.

Using IPT Results at the School Level

A frequent but sometimes misguided summative use of test scores involves ranking and evaluating teachers, classes, schools, districts, and states. There are caveats when using test results for these purposes. The College Board's flagship assessment, the SAT, is an example. The College Board has warned that "using aggregate SAT scores to compare or evaluate teachers, schools, districts, states or other educational units is not valid, and the College Board strongly discourages such uses."[21] Unfortunately, such uses of test scores are all too common.

Fair comparisons between the IPT results of different schools are possible, provided the demographic characteristics of the schools' fourth- or seventh-grade populations are comparable, and test preparation, administration procedures, and scoring processes are essentially the same. Fair comparisons have allowed VBCPS building administrators and teachers to see where they stand in relation to other schools in the district. IPT scores are not about bragging rights or ranking schools in the district. Rather, school-level results are used to start conversations and plan instruction in areas where improvement is needed.

A few years ago, a researcher wanted to find out how seventh-grade IPT results were being used at middle schools. By analyzing documents that each school was required to submit to the central office after the fall administration, the researcher determined (1) the ways that teachers at nine middle schools used students' IPT responses to inform instruction, and (2) how students at the schools reflected on their responses and scores.[22]

The analysis indicated that building administrators, classroom teachers, and resource specialists met in professional learning communities (PLCs) to review IPT results and plan instruction. PLCs at three schools looked at school averages and trends for CT, PS, and WC scores, while PLCs at the other schools evaluated a number of seventh-grade responses selected at random. The latter method incorporated formal data analysis protocols that offered insights into student performance related to deeper learning skills.

The schools subsequently instituted various instructional strategies and activities to promote critical thinking, problem solving, and effective writing. Teachers implemented or increased the use of document-based questions (DBQs); interdisciplinary performance tasks; persuasive writing prompts; the role, audience, format, and topic strategy (RAFTS); and Socratic seminars. Although some strategies, such as DBQs and RAFTS, were limited to specific subjects, other instructional methods were employed across core subject areas and in elective and special area classes.

Different methods of sharing IPT results with students were used at the schools. In several buildings, teachers showed their students sample responses at the *novice, emerging, proficient,* and *advanced* levels. By examining the sample responses, students became adept at interpreting the rubric relative to their own scores. Teachers at other schools handed out students' scored responses for their classes to reread. The students were asked to self-assess and consider ways they could improve their performance on future performance tasks, including the CWRA. At some schools, students worked collaboratively with peers to review, discuss, and improve their written answers.

The researcher and her coauthor concluded that the IPT led to positive instructional changes at VBCPS middle schools. They asserted, "Performance assessment has the potential to change teaching on a scale that curricular revisions and typical professional development activities cannot achieve."[23] Richard Paul and Linda Elder, two prominent critical-thinking authorities, would probably agree. Paul and Elder argued that quality assessments of critical thinking lead to the utilization of critical-thinking strategies in the classroom simply because teachers want their students to do well on the assessments.[24] Put another way, assessment drives instruction.

Incorporating the Five Cs

The most recent change to the IPT occurred after the Virginia Department of Education (VDOE) announced it would adopt new standards for earning a high school diploma. The new standards, now in effect for students who will graduate in 2022, include the *Profile of a Virginia Graduate*, a document that reflects "the knowledge, skills, attributes and experiences identified by employers, higher education and the state Board of Education as critical for future success."[25] The VDOE requires Virginia schools to prepare students by developing their competency in the five Cs: critical thinking, creative thinking, communication, collaboration, and citizenship.

With the new high school graduation standards looming, the chief academic officer (CAO) of VBCPS arranged a meeting with staff responsible for IPT development, which, by the time, was down to one educational measurement and assessment specialist. The CAO suggested incorporating the five Cs in the next batch of IPTs. Since the existing tasks measured critical thinking and communication, the new tasks would also need to address creativity, collaboration, and citizenship.

The actual measurement of creative thinking and collaboration would require a major overhaul to the IPT—something we were not prepared to do—but it was possible to work these Cs into IPT-related classroom lessons. A few savvy VBCPS teachers were already fostering the two skills through creative and collaborative post-task activities. An activity that facilitated creative thinking involved students coming up with original solutions to the problem posed by an IPT situation. For collaboration, students worked in small groups to brainstorm and discuss the solutions. They also reviewed and evaluated each other's responses in collaborative groups, as mentioned in the study described earlier.

Adding a citizenship indicator to the new IPTs was imminently doable, and accomplished by developing situations that involved minor ethical dilemmas—incidents fourth- or seventh-grade students might encounter at school. The grade 4 situations deal with telling the truth and privacy, while the issues for grade 7 are bullying and theft. Like the previous tasks, the new IPTs include documents with evidence meant to steer students toward the more socially responsible choice.

Because the new IPTs feature an indicator of citizenship (they don't actually *measure* citizenship), teachers who examine their class's responses are able to see how their students react to a hypothetical quandary that has an apparent best answer. Sometimes students don't choose wisely because they haven't read some or all of the documents. Occasionally, a student's response contains ill-advised reasoning for choosing wrongly. If a teacher is aware of such a response, she can act as a positive influence on the social-emotional development of the student.

When teachers read their students' IPT responses, they gain an understanding of how each student thinks, processes information, and formulates ideas into writing. Combined with what they already know about their students, the information that teachers garner from IPT responses enhances their ability to plan and deliver instruction for deeper learning. Accordingly, IPT responses are much more valuable than IPT scores for teachers to use formatively in the classroom.

SUMMARY

The CWRA and CLA have long been touted as tests worth teaching to. The same is true for the IPT. Conventional pedagogy involves a circular process of teaching, testing, and planning for the next cycle. With performance tasks, deeper learning and assessment happen simultaneously. When performance tasks are used regularly, "students will not only master the content knowledge and skills for a particular course, . . . they will also gain the practice they need to be better critical thinkers when they face novel scenarios or problems, either within the same domain or across domains."[26]

Chapter 8 addressed the reliability and validity of IPT results and how the results are used by educators in Virginia Beach. Using results from the IPT can advance deeper learning in ways that are analogous to the use of CWRA results, by "help[ing] administrators and teachers discuss in more explicit and transparent ways how their pedagogy, curriculum, and assessment can be improved to teach such skills across subjects and grades."[27]

Here are three general takeaways from this chapter:

- Every assessment should have, at a minimum, content-related evidence of validity as an indication that its scores are valid for their intended purposes. Assessments whose results are used to make high-stakes decisions require additional evidence of validity.

- Although performance task results can be used summatively by schools and districts, using the results formatively in classrooms can have an immediate, beneficial impact on students' deeper learning.
- Performance tasks facilitate concurrent learning and assessment, with students becoming proficient at deeper learning skills at the same time they demonstrate the skills.

At this point in the book, the benefits of using performance tasks should be obvious. Promoting deeper learning through the use of performance assessment is not a new idea, but it has gained steam recently. In the next chapter, Chris Gareis discusses the classroom use of performance assessments in different subjects and at different grade levels.

NOTES

1. American Educational Research Association (AERA), American Psychological Association (APA), and National Council for Measurement in Education (NCTM), *Standards for Educational and Psychological Testing* (Washington, DC: American Educational Research Association, 2014), 222–23.

2. Susan M. Brookhart, "Developing Measurement Theory for Classroom Assessment Purposes and Uses," *Educational Measurement: Issues and Practice* 22, no. 4 (December 2003), 5.

3. Joan L. Herman, Ellen Osmundson, and Ronald Dietel, *Benchmark Assessment for Improved Learning* (Los Angeles: University of California, 2010), 4.

4. W. James Popham, "Face Validity: Siren Song for Teacher Testers," in *Assessment of Teaching: Purposes, Practices, and Implications for the Profession*, ed. James Y. Mitchell, Jr., Steven L. Wise, and Barbara S. Plake (Hillsdale, NJ: Lawrence Erlbaum Associates, 1990), 2.

5. Charles Secolsky, "On the Direct Measurement of Face Validity: A Comment on Nevo," *Journal of Educational Measurement* 24, no. 1 (Spring 1987), 82.

6. AERA, APA, and NCTM, 14.

7. Samuel L. Messick, *Validity of Test Interpretation and Use* (Princeton, NJ: Educational Testing Service, 1990), 5, ERIC, ED 395031.

8. Ibid., 8.

9. Justin Brady, "The Troubling Flaws in How We Select Experts," *Washington Post*, June 25, 2014, https://www.washingtonpost.com/news/innovations/wp/2014/06/25/the-troubling-flaws-in-how-we-select-experts/?utm_term=.cddf0d5a8496.

10. David Allen Payne, *Applied Educational Assessment*, 2nd ed. (Belmont, CA: Wadsworth Thomson Learning, 2003), 412.

11. Marc Chun, "Taking Teaching to (Performance) Task: Linking Pedagogical and Assessment Practices," *Change: The Magazine of Higher Learning* 42, no. 2 (March/April 2010), 24.

12. Linda Crocker and James Algina, *Introduction to Classical and Modern Test Theory* (Holt, Rinehart and Winston, 1986), 224–25.

13. Ibid., 225.

14. Insight Assessment, "California Critical Thinking Skills Test, CCTST Overview," 2018, https://www.insightassessment.com/Products/Products-Summary/Critical-Thinking-Skills-Tests/California-Critical-Thinking-Skills-Test-CCTST.

15. James H. MacMillan and Sally Schumaker, *Research in Education*, 5th ed. (New York: Addison Wesley Longman, 2001), 176.

16. Crocker and Algina, 226.

17. Lee J. Cronbach, *Essentials of Psychological Testing*, 3rd ed. (New York: Harper & Row, 1970), 135.

18. Ibid.

19. All eight correlation coefficients in table 8.1 were statistically significant at the .01 alpha level, meaning the probability of the results occurring by chance was less than 1 percent.

20. AERA, APA, and NCTM, 216.

21. College Board, *2016 College-Bound Seniors Total Group Profile Report*, ii.

22. Amy L. Abbott and Douglas G. Wren, "Using Performance Task Data to Improve Instruction," *The Clearing House: A Journal of Educational Strategies, Issues and Ideas* 89, no. 1 (2016), 38–40.

23. Ibid., 43.

24. Richard Paul and Linda Elder, "Consequential Validity: Using Assessment to Drive Instruction," 2007, 7, http://www.criticalthinking.org/files/White%20PaperAssessmentSept2007.pdf.

25. Virginia Department of Education, *In Brief: Graduation Requirements*, June 2018, http://www.doe.virginia.gov/boe/accreditation/grad-req.pdf.

26. Chun, 24.

27. Richard H. Hersh, "Life Is Not a Standardized Test," January 2001, 2, https://www.educationevolving.org/pdf/Life_not_a_standardized_test.pdf.

Chapter 9

Leveraging Performance Assessment in the Classroom

Chris Gareis

The main focus of this book is the design, development, and use of performance tasks at the district level; however, as alluded to in our opening chapter, the use of performance tasks by teachers at the classroom level is an essential element of a balanced approach to assessment. In this chapter, we describe ways to leverage the use of performance tasks in the classroom, particularly from the broader perspective of using performance-based assessments as part of the teaching and learning process.

By leverage, we are suggesting how one might exert strategic, purposeful, focused effort on something one is already doing. In this case, we mean implementing performance assessments in order to achieve another important goal—namely, more engaged instruction and deeper learning outcomes.

We begin by revisiting the notion of balanced assessment for classroom teachers and then introduce examples of common types of performance assessments. Next, we consider several concrete actions that teachers and instructional leaders can take to leverage performance assessments for teaching and learning in classrooms.

BALANCED CLASSROOM ASSESSMENT

The term *classroom assessment* refers to the use of assessment practices by teachers at the classroom level for purposes of teaching and learning.[1] The need to distinguish this term from the term *assessment* alone was recognized more than thirty years ago as researchers determined that knowledge of and expertise in assessment were a relative weakness among many classroom teachers and school-level leaders.[2] This weakness became accentuated in more recent times as the accountability era ramped up the need for teachers to be proficient not only in analyzing the results of standardized assessments but also in creating and using more appropriate assessment practices at the classroom level.[3]

Even more recently, the need to develop teachers' capacity for effective classroom assessment practices has expanded as the aim of developing twenty-first-century skills, college and career readiness, and deeper learning outcomes for students has gained prominence. As previously discussed, conventional, selected-response types of assessments such as multiple-choice and technology-enhanced items play an important role when a teacher needs to gauge the nature and degree of learning about a breadth of content at lower and middle levels of cognitive rigor in an efficient and objective manner.

However, when the teacher's need is to assess students' ability to persist at a task over time, to draw upon a depth of subject-area understanding, and to engage with that content through inferential analysis, evaluation, and synthesis in novel and authentic situations, performance assessments are needed. A teacher's use of both conventional and performance-based assessments constitutes an important dimension of a balanced approach to assessment, and the principle of balanced assessment is germane to all teachers, whether teaching kindergartners, tweens, teens, or young adults and whether teaching English, mathematics, studio arts, physics, or the culinary art of perfecting a soufflé.

PERFORMANCE ASSESSMENTS ACROSS THE CURRICULUM

While balanced assessment should characterize the assessment practices of every teacher, the use of performance assessment is quite likely to vary across the curriculum. To begin with, not all performance assessments are of one type. Performance assessments vary by at least four characteristics:

1. the number of intended learning outcomes to which they are aligned;
2. the degree to which the teacher is involved in students' completion of the performance assessment;
3. the prescriptiveness of the response; and
4. the duration of time required for completion.

Variations in these four characteristics constitute four commonly recognized types of performance assessments that teachers can use in the classroom. These characteristics and types of performance assessments are outlined in table 9.1, and we offer brief examples and explanations of each.[4]

Table 9.1 Characteristics and types of performance assessment

Characteristics	Types of Performance Assessments			
	Constructed Response	Stand-Alone	Unit-Embedded	Complex Project
• number of intended learning outcomes (ILOs)	• 1–2 ILOs	• multiple, subject-specific ILOs	• a cogent set of subject-specific ILOs	• a complex, integrative set of ILOs and broad aims
• level of instructional support from teacher during administration	• limited to clarification	• limited clarification and facilitation	• integrated instruction, facilitation, and feedback	• integrated instruction, facilitation, feedback, and guidance
• prescriptiveness of student response (degree of student choice)	• fixed/convergent (typically little choice)	• convergent (limited choice)	• moderately Divergent (elements of choice in content and/or format of response)	• divergent (typically multiple opportunities for student choice)
• zpproximate duration	• a portion of a class period (≤ 60 minutes)	• 1–2 class periods (> 60 minutes)	• multiple class periods or days	• multiple weeks or a term

Adapted from Stanford Center for Assessment and Learning Equity (SCALE).

Constructed-Response Performance Assessments

Constructed-response performance assessments are designed to have students demonstrate proficiency in one or two intended learning outcomes, with limited guidance from the teacher, in a format that allows for only moderate student choice, and typically takes only minutes to complete.

For example, third-grade students may be given a set of mock data from a long jump competition and prompted to respond to a series of questions that require them to apply their number sense, addition and subtraction skills, and mathematical reasoning. Students' responses in this example take the form of numeric answers and short, written explanations of their reasoning. Although students are determining and writing (rather than selecting) their own numeric answers as well as deciding how to express their reasoning in their own short, written responses, the actual degree of choice in how they respond is quite limited. Also, the numeric answers clearly have correct responses that require merely an answer key for the teacher to mark; even the written response is narrow in the range of possible correct responses.

Constructed-response performance assessments are a staple of a balanced approach to assessment. Because of their focused, efficient structure, they can be used to quickly measure discrete intended learning outcomes while tapping higher-order thinking. Because they are limited in the number of objectives that they assess, constructed-response items tend to be an effective means of formatively assessing student learning during a lesson.

For the same reason, constructed-response items are limited in their utility when used individually as part of a formal assessment. Typically, when assessing student learning, teachers will use a series of constructed-response items that can be taken together to demonstrate a complex set of student learning outcomes. Indeed, a familiar practice to most teachers is to use constructed-response items in combination with conventional, selected-response assessment items such as multiple choice and matching in order to get a comprehensive view of student learning.

From performance tasks used to gauge student learning during a lesson to the use of a structured sequence of open-ended responses on a summative test, constructed-response items have broad utility. What's more, their utility extends across grade levels and subject areas, as illustrated by examples such as these:

- Middle school history students are presented three examples of historical sources and are then prompted to identify each as either a primary or secondary source and explain their conclusion in a single paragraph for each, based upon specific characteristics of each source (e.g., date, author, format of source).

- High school biology students are provided a scenario involving a genetic trait and its line of heredity. Individually, they analyze the scenario, create an accurate and complete Punnett square to illustrate the scenario, and then create a visual tree model to depict possible outcomes given additional sets of variables.
- Secondary students in an introductory culinary arts course are introduced to, review examples of, and engage in scenarios involving the construct of *mise en place* (which translates as *everything in its place* and is a foundational understanding and skill in food preparation). To assess students' understanding of the principles of *mise en place*, the teacher gives students a series of visual depictions of private and professional kitchens and has students identify examples and nonexamples of *mise en place* in the pictures.

Again, the distinguishing features of constructed-response performance assessments are the limited number of targeted intended learning outcomes, the limited degree of student choice, the limited involvement of the teacher in providing guidance or feedback in completing the actual task, and the limited duration of time needed to complete it. Also notable is that a constructed-response item is typically used in conjunction with other constructed-response or selected-response items in order to create a broader representation of student learning.

Stand-Alone Performance Assessments

Whereas constructed-response performance assessments are generally used in conjunction with other assessment items, *stand-alone* performance assessments—as the name suggests—are designed to function by themselves as means of assessing complex sets of intended learning outcomes, usually involving multiple objectives.

Teachers tend to play a limited role in students' completion of stand-alone performance assessments, although the complexity of the prompt may require teacher guidance and possibly some degree of facilitation. Because stand-alone assessments are typically intended to be completed over the course of an instructional period or two (although most commonly in a single sitting), the degree of choice for students tends to be limited to the content of a student's response rather than to the format or the process by which that student responds.

A common type of stand-alone performance assessment is the essay test. Such an assessment might consist of a single essay prompt intended to tap into a depth of content knowledge, to necessitate higher-order thinking, and to require proficiency in a mode of written communication. Of course, what is meant by essay will vary by grade level, subject area, and purpose. For instance, a single, well-constructed paragraph might constitute a developmentally appropriate format for third-grade students, whereas middle-grades students might be expected to compose a conventional three-paragraph essay, and secondary students might be expected to compose a paper framed by the number of pages rather than the discrete number of paragraphs.

What also varies among essay-type, stand-alone performance assessments is the purpose of the writing and, therefore, the form that the written piece may take. For example, the purpose of an academic essay may be to describe, to inform, to explain, to argue, or to persuade, each of which involves different conventions of format, tone, and techniques.

But not all such prompts need be academic in nature. Because a distinguishing feature of performance assessments is that they may tap into authentic scenarios, an essay might take the form of a descriptive memoir, an explanatory newspaper article, a fictional narrative account, an entry in a technical manual, an argumentative case, or a persuasive letter. Whether such prompts are academic or scenario-based, stand-alone assessments are oftentimes used to tap into modes of communication (such as the varied forms of writing just referred to) that are intended learning outcomes themselves.

Not all stand-alone performance assessments, though, are essays. In the sciences, a common type of stand-alone performance assessment is the lab practical. While lab practicals may take many different forms, they typically represent a complex set of knowledge and skills, are completed within a standard instructional period, and involve students circulating among stations at which they perform different tasks and respond to various prompts.

Another form of stand-alone performance assessments is the oral exam, which can be used across a range of subject areas. Oral exams are particularly important to use when the oral expression of reasoning is an intended learning outcome. Frankly, in our experience, the intentional teaching and assessing of oral language competencies is often minimized, forgotten, or ignored in K–12 public education, yet a review of standards documents reveals the presence of objectives related to the oral expression of understanding and reasoning across grade levels and subject areas.[5] With the call for ensuring that every student in the twenty-first century is an effective communicator, the periodic and intentional use of stand-alone oral exams is surely justified.

Unit-Embedded Performance Assessments

A third type of performance assessment is characterized by being situated within a unit of instruction and is therefore referred to as *unit-embedded*. Such assessments are designed to prompt students to demonstrate a cogent set of intended learning outcomes—that is to say, a complex but coherent set of knowledge and subject-specific skills that are applied over an extended period of time, whether several days or even a week or more. The complexity of the intended learning outcomes and the extended nature of such tasks tend to necessitate the integration of instruction into the performance assessment, wherein the teacher directs and facilitates students' work and may even provide corrective feedback over a limited span of time.

Examples of possible unit-embedded performance assessments abound. In a geometry class, for instance, students are given a scenario that charges them to take on the role of packaging engineers who must design a structurally stable box that makes optimal use of cardboard packaging material and is used for shipping fruit juice cartons. From the introduction of the task to its completion, students are prompted to brainstorm designs, apply their understanding of geometry, learn new geometric principles, collaborate with others, and engage in mathematical reasoning and communication. The complexity, applied nature, and authenticity of the task requires the guidance, facilitation, and, at times, direct instruction of the teacher, reflective of characteristics of deeper learning.

In foreign language classes, unit-embedded performance assessments are a staple of effective pedagogy as teachers make use of integrated performance assessments. Drawing on the content and skills of a given unit, such as a unit on travel, leisure activities, the business place, or food preparation, a teacher devises a series of performance assessments that tap into various authentic modes of communication. These might typically include speaking and listening, reading and writing, and creating and interpreting digital or visual media, such as posters or graphics. Clearly, each of these modes is relevant to proficient communication in a foreign language, but their complex and varied nature necessitates the demonstration of the modes in integrative ways.

As another example of a unit-embedded performance assessment, a visual arts teacher may make use of the classic instructional method of having students study and then paint in the style of a master artist. Clearly, the act of painting itself suggests a more extended performance task characteristic of unit-embedded assessments. However, it is during such production that the teacher monitors elements of composition and technique, poses questions to students, provides guidance, and deepens students' understanding of the artist and their own application of the master's techniques. For instance, the teacher may prompt students' deeper thinking by asking, "How has painting in the style of this master expanded your self-expression as an artist, and how has it inhibited your self-expression?" Again, the complexity, authenticity, and time intensity of this physical and intellectual task necessitate a unit-embedded approach to assessment.

Complex Projects

A fourth type of performance assessment is the *complex project*. Complex projects are designed to engage students in tasks that require them to draw upon distinct knowledge and skills from multiple disciplines. Complex projects are also particularly amenable to providing evidence of some of the broader aims of education, such as critical thinking, creative problem solving, effective communication, and constructive collaboration—namely, deeper learning.[6]

Similar to unit-embedded performance assessments, complex projects depend upon a teacher's integrated instruction, facilitation, guidance, and feedback. However, due to the complex nature of the task, such instruction is not anchored in a single unit of study and, due to the extended nature of the product being developed, such facilitation typically must occur at varied times and milestones in the process.

A particular feature of complex projects is the considerable degree of student agency that is exercised in undertaking the project. Students might choose their own topics and even their own purpose in pursuing the project. They may have wide latitude in making decisions about the means or process of undertaking the project. Students might identify the most relevant and useful products or outcomes of the project. Indeed, the very criteria by which student performance is assessed on the project may vary student to student.

As an example, students might undertake researching the first public school for African American students in a segregated county, identifying its location, revealing its history from founding to closing, learning about its students and teachers, investigating its struggles, and gauging its significance to the present-day community. Their application of research skills, historical analyses, economics, geography, communication, collaboration, and civic-mindedness may result in a formal written and oral proposal to a local governing body to establish a historical marker on the site of the school. The authenticity and relevance of such a project is clear. What's more, the fluid, unpredictable nature of the work should also be evident to any teacher who has ever attempted to undertake this sort of student-driven learning experience, commonly known as project-based learning.[7]

But it also warrants pointing out that not all complex projects need be so open ended or relevant to current issues. Consider the classic high school term paper, which might occur, for instance, in a history course. Effective teachers are able to carefully orchestrate complex, rigorous, applied processes from students' selection of topics to researching, analyzing, synthesizing, and positing meaningful ideas and then prewriting, drafting, revising, editing, and finalizing the formal paper itself. In other words, complex projects can be tightly aligned to sets of academic standards and effectively facilitated, leading to the efficient but rigorous completion of the project.

QUALITIES OF WELL-DESIGNED PERFORMANCE ASSESSMENTS

Referring again to table 9.1, performance assessments can be distinguished by the number of intended learning outcomes to which they are aligned, the role of the teacher in facilitating students' undertaking of the performance task, the degree of student choice and prescriptiveness of response, and the duration of time needed for the task. These four defining characteristics are best thought of as a continuum, suggesting various possible iterations of each characteristic that can be broadly categorized as constructed-response, stand-alone, unit-embedded, and complex projects.

Regardless of the type, all quality performance assessments should be characterized by a set of common criteria, which we offer in table 9.2.[8] With

Table 9.2 Quality criteria for performance assessments

1. Aligns to a *cogent set of intended learning outcomes* (typically involving a depth of content knowledge with subject-specific skills).
2. Requires students to engage in *higher-order thinking* over some extended period of time (whether several minutes or multiple weeks).
3. Engages students in an *authentic task* that is representative of the real world and/or relevant to the academic discipline.
4. Initiates and guides the student's performance with a *prompt* (and other *student-facing materials*, as needed) that is clear, coherent, developmentally appropriate, and clearly aligned to the criteria being assessed.
5. Requires a *response format* (i.e., performance and/or product) that is relevant to the intended learning outcomes and feasible within the parameters of curricular pacing, available resources, and prior student learning.
6. Requires the student's *verbal expression of reasoning* such as through writing, speaking, or other modes of communication (e.g., graphic representation, digitally based), thereby supporting language development and thinking.
7. Evaluates the student's performance and/or product using *accurate, reasonably objective criteria*, typically in the form of a rubric.
8. Allows for *accessibility to all students* by identifying appropriate, allowable supports or alternatives to facilitate engagement while maintaining the validity and reliability of the performance assessment.
9. Necessitates *instructional strategies or methods* that engage students in deeper learning.
10. Provides *substantive information and clear directions to teachers* (and other *teacher-facing materials*, as needed) to ensure fidelity of instruction, administration, scoring, and use.

the intent of designing and developing performance assessments that will progress deeper learning, we would contend that these quality criteria should be evident in performance assessments across all grade levels and subject areas.

The criteria for quality performance assessments are anchored in an understanding of the principles of deeper learning and psychometrics. For example, the first, second, and third criteria articulate the need for content mastery, higher-order thinking skills, and authenticity, each of which is reflective of the first three principles of deeper learning described in chapter 1. The requirement for alignment, on the other hand, is reflective of the psychometric property of validity, which can be thought of as the degree to which an assessment can lead to appropriate inferences about intended student learning.[9]

Similarly, the fifth, sixth, and ninth criteria are concerned with elements of deeper learning, namely the format of the performance students are undertaking and/or the products they are creating through the performance assessment; the students' verbal articulation of their reasoning; and the necessity of high-yield, engaging instructional methods to facilitate deeper learning.

As complementary elements, the fourth, seventh, eighth, and tenth criteria concentrate more on psychometric principles associated with the design and development of assessments, namely the clarity and accuracy of the performance prompt, the creation and use of rubrics for accurately and fairly evaluating student performance, the accessibility of the performance assessment to all learners, and the concerted effort to better ensure the appropriate administration and use of performance assessments and their results.

Taken as a whole, this set of criteria can be used as a kind of checklist to guide the development of performance assessments. The quality criteria can also be used to judge the potential quality of performance assessments that a teacher or team of teachers is considering adopting. The point is that performance assessments must be more than fun, engaging activities in the classroom—although fun and engagement are extraordinarily worthwhile qualities of teaching! Performance assessments should be designed such that they promote deeper learning and yield results that are valid, reliable indicators of deeper learning outcomes.

LEVERAGING PERFORMANCE ASSESSMENTS

Performance assessments can also be leveraged to achieve other important educational aims. Here we address three such aims that we believe are both broadly relevant and of particular importance: improving student literacy, promoting STEM careers, and engaging students in their own learning.

Improving Student Literacy

The role of literacy in educational and work-life outcomes is undeniable. The capacity to think, to learn, and to communicate is utterly dependent upon language. The bedrock of language is literacy, which can be defined as the ability to read and write in order to get along in the world. However, as important as literacy is, the United States continues to confront low literacy rates.[10] The issue is compounded by increasing economic disparities and by increasing populations of students who are learning English as a second language (ESL). Consequently, many school districts have identified ensuring the basic literacy of all students as a strategic goal.[11]

Anchored in communication as a goal of deeper learning, the use of performance assessments can be used to leverage language development among students. Quality performance assessments typically require students to undertake a process and create a product, and quality performance assessments also require students' verbal expression of reasoning through writing, speaking, or other modes of communication (e.g., graphic representation or digitally based). Accessing multiple means of communication provides experiences that are authentic to language use and development.

Further, different types of performance assessments (such as constructed-response and complex projects) and the authentic nature of specific performance tasks can support students' use and development of language. For example, academic tasks require students to access and make use of disciplinary vocabulary and language conventions while scenario-based tasks prompt and support the use of functional literacy, social language production, and expression, whether through conversation, text, or media. Accentuating the role of verbal reasoning in the design and use of performance assessments can be a way to improve student literacy while teaching for deeper learning.

Promoting STEM Careers

Performance assessments also can be leveraged to promote students' knowledge of and interest in careers in STEM. The call to draw more students to and strengthen their preparation in STEM subjects has been concomitant to national and international initiatives to prepare twenty-first-century students who are career and college ready and who are also well prepared to thrive in and contribute to human innovation. Anchored in mastery of core content, higher-order thinking, complex problem solving, authentic tasks, and growth mind-sets, performance assessments are necessary for the development of the sorts of knowledge, skills, and dispositions that characterize STEM subject and fields.

In short, if a school or district has a STEM initiative in place, then performance assessments are a necessary component of a systemic and intentional approach to achieving STEM goals. We should note, though, that leveraging performance assessments for STEM careers is not unique to STEM alone. For the same reasons we cited previously, performance assessments are a means of promoting students' exploration and movement toward all manner of career goals, whether they be in law, education, culinary arts, performance arts, business, or other non-STEM fields.

Accentuating the breadth and depth of subject knowledge and making intentional use of authentic tasks in the design and use of performance assessments can be a way to leverage them to support career and college readiness in all fields.

Engaging Students in Their Own Learning

As alluded to in the previous discussion of quality criteria, performance assessments have the potential to promote instruction that is engaging and motivating for students. Grounded in deeper learning outcomes of authenticity and learning how to learn, performance assessments can be designed to engage students cognitively, affectively, and even physically. These three domains of human behavior constitute not only the domains of intended learning outcomes (i.e., what we want students to know, to be motivated by, and to actively engage with) but also the means to those outcomes.

Another way to think of the relationship between performance assessments and engaging students in learning is to consider this fundamental premise: *how* a teacher decides to teach students should be premised on *what* it is that the teacher wants his or her students to learn. In short, instruction should be aligned to curriculum.[12] Continuing with this basic premise, if our aim is deeper learning that involves mastery of core content and higher-order thinking, then our instruction needs to emphasize core content and to prompt and support students' use and development of higher-order thinking skills.

What kinds of instructional methods and strategies tend to promote deeper learning? In table 9.3, we offer a number of examples, each of which has a convincing basis in research.[13] What characterizes each of these methods is that they use the authentic, discipline-specific skills of the subjects themselves as the means of engaging students in and thereby developing deeper learning.

Furthermore, each of these instructional methods requires both active participation by students and some degree of cognitive, affective, and even physical engagement. Still further, each of these instructional methods can be designed to allow for varying degrees of student choice (which can be

Table 9.3 Examples of instructional methods that promote student engagement and deeper learning

Subjects	Exemplary Instructional Methods
Science	• inquiry teaching
English Language Arts	• readers' workshop • writers' workshop
History/Social Studies	• Socratic discussions • jurisprudential inquiry • debate • simulations (e.g., mock economies, moot court, mock/student elections) • cooperative learning
Mathematics	• math workshop • problem-based learning
any subject	• project-based learning

motivating), interpersonal interaction (which can also be motivating), and challenge (which, too, can be motivating!).

The examples we have offered are specific to four core subjects, with the exception of the final example of project-based learning. It is important to reiterate that these are illustrative examples and certainly are not exhaustive of all instructional methods that elicit student engagement and deeper learning. Other effective methods exist in these subjects and in other subjects.

However, it is also important to note that we have not simply identified every instructional strategy and technique that has evidence of effectiveness. For example, the use of cues as a strategy has been demonstrated to have a positive effect on some learning outcomes, but cuing itself is not a model of instruction that would elicit deeper learning.[14] The same is true of certain teaching techniques, such as drawing Popsicle sticks with student names on them as a technique for randomly calling on students and ensuring broad participation.[15] While a useful technique, it alone is not sufficient to result in deeper learning outcomes.

In short, if we want deeper learning outcomes for our students, our teaching needs to engage them more deeply, more authentically, and more personally. By their very nature of having students *think* and *do*, performance assessments can be leveraged for student engagement and deeper learning.

SUMMARY

If our educational aims are to prepare students for the challenges and opportunities of the twenty-first century, then we need to teach—and assess—for deeper learning. When they are well designed, performance assessments can effectively and meaningfully assess deeper learning outcomes. When created and used by teachers in the classroom, performance assessments can themselves become drivers of deeper learning.

A common criticism of the era of high-stakes standardized testing is that many teachers have been pressed to teach to the test. Frankly, there is nothing wrong with teaching to the test. For example, to obtain a driver's license, you have to successfully complete both a written test of knowledge and an on-the-road test of applied knowledge and skills. Teaching to these important outcomes just makes sense!

And therein lies the insidious, unintended consequence of the use of standardized accountability assessments in education: they have caused many educators to prepare students for tests that are by themselves insufficient measures of some of our most important educational aims. Performance assessments are the necessary balance to the use of conventional assessments. Simply put, performance assessments are tests worth teaching to because they serve as both a means to and an indicator of deeper learning.

In this chapter, the focus was on the use of performance assessments at the classroom level and the following takeaways:

- Teaching and learning in classrooms—regardless of grade level or subject area—requires a balanced approach to assessment.
- While all performance assessments have students engage in higher-order thinking and produce evidence of knowledge, understanding, and skills, performance assessments can differ in their complexity, degree of divergence, time to complete, and other characteristics. Therefore, it is important to know and use different types of performance assessments, namely constructed-response, stand-alone, unit-embedded, and complex projects.
- Selecting and creating valid and reliable performance assessments for use in the classroom requires professional knowledge about the characteristics of quality performance assessments.
- Performance assessments—and the authentic tasks that typify them—can be leveraged to teach for deeper learning, promote language and literacy development, promote STEM careers, and foster student engagement in learning. In short, performance assessments are not merely assessments *of* learning but assessments *for* learning.

NOTES

1. Christopher R. Gareis and Leslie W. Grant, *Teacher-Made Assessments: How to Connect Curriculum, Instruction, and Student Learning*, 2nd ed. (New York: Routledge, 2015).

2. Richard J. Stiggins and Nancy Faires Conklin, *In Teachers' Hands: Investigating the Practices of Classroom Assessment* (Albany: State University of New York Press, 1992).

3. Gareis and Grant; Lorrie Shepard, foreword to *Handbook of Research on Classroom Assessment* (Thousand Oaks, CA: SAGE Publications, 2013).

4. Stanford Center for Assessment and Learning Equity (SCALE). "Other Resources," December 16, 2018, https://www.performanceassessmentresourcebank.org/other-resources.

5. See, for example, Foreign Language Teachers Association, National Council for the Social Studies, National Council of Teacher of English, and National Council of Teachers of Mathematics.

6. Bernie Trilling and Charles Fadel, *21st Century Skills: Learning for Life in Our Times* (San Francisco: Jossey-Bass, 2012).

7. John Larmer, John Mergendoller, and Suzie Boss, *Setting the Standard for Project Based Learning: A Proven Approach to Rigorous Classroom Instruction* (Alexandria, VA: Association for Supervision and Curriculum Development, 2015).

8. Christopher R. Gareis, "Exploring the Intersectionality of Performance Assessments: Crossroads, Crosswords, and Crosshairs" (keynote presentation, 27th Annual Conference of the Consortium for Research on Educational Assessment and Teaching Effectiveness, Williamsburg, VA, October 11, 2018).

9. Gareis and Grant.

10. National Center for Education Statistics, "Average Literacy and Numeracy Scale Scores and Percentage Distribution of 25- to 65-Year-Olds, by Proficiency Level and Selected Characteristics: 2012/2014," https://nces.ed.gov/programs/digest/d16/tables/dt16_507.15.asp.

11. Noel G. Williams, Leah S. Horrell, and Davis Clement, *Constructing the Language of Reform: Deficit Discourse in District-Level Policy Implementation* (paper presented at the 40th Annual Conference of the Eastern Educational Research Association, Richmond, VA, February 24, 2017).

12. Gareis and Grant; Grant Wiggins and Jay McTighe, *Understanding by Design*, 2nd ed. (Alexandria, VA: Association for Supervision and Curriculum Development, 2005).

13. Bruce R. Joyce, Emily Calhoun, and Marsha Weil, *Models of Teaching*, 9th ed. (Boston: Pearson, 2015); Robert J. Marzano, Debra J. Pickering, and Jane E. Pollock, *Classroom Instruction That Works: Research-Based Strategies for Increasing Student Achievement* (Alexandria, VA: Association for Supervision and Curriculum Development, 2001); John Hattie, *Visible Learning: A Synthesis of Over 800 Meta-Analyses Relating to Achievement* (New York: Routledge, 2009).

14. Marzano, Pickering, and Pollock.

Chapter 10

Purposeful Innovation

Chris Gareis

The purpose of this book has been to add our voices to the chorus of those calling for deeper learning. More specifically, we have set out not only to advocate for but also to illustrate how to design, develop, and use performance tasks as part of a meaningful, useful balanced approach to teaching, learning, assessment, and accountability. In this chapter, we offer additional perspectives on the importance of this move and explore a few factors that we contend are essential to purposefully undertaking such an innovation.

IT'S TIME

The premise of assessing for deeper learning begins with first understanding what *deeper learning* is. We unpacked this in chapter 1 and identified seven intended outcomes that serve as the aims of deeper learning, namely mastering core content, thinking critically, solving complex problems, working collaboratively, communicating effectively, learning how to learn, and developing an academic mind-set.[1] With these outcomes in mind, the most appropriate means of assessing such learning leads logically to the use of performance tasks.

While the articulation of *deeper learning* as a construct is relatively new, the call for the use of performance assessments is not. As a case in point, consider this quotation: "We need a new philosophy of assessment in this country that never loses sight of the student. To build such an assessment, we need to return to the roots of authentic assessment, the assessment of performance of exemplary tasks."[2] This quotation is instructive for several reasons. First, it begins by asserting the importance of assessing student learning in ways that keep *student* and *learning* at the heart of assessment practices. Second, it pointedly identifies *performance tasks* as being central to such an approach to assessment. Finally, it suggests that the use of performance assessments *is not new*.

The author of the quotation is Grant Wiggins, who wrote this in the journal *Phi Delta Kappan* in the late 1980s. With this in mind, we recognize that the title of this chapter, "Purposeful Innovation," may be a misnomer. After all, how can something from the past be considered an innovation in the present?

We see it this way: The move toward the full realization of performance assessment is an interrupted innovation. Wiggins pointed this out in 1989 by calling out "the need to return to the roots of authentic assessment," suggesting previous eras when performance tasks had been part of effective pedagogy. In other words, the innovative use of performance tasks had been previously interrupted, and Wiggins prompted a refocusing on it back in 1989.

As we described in chapter 2, the decade of the 1990s saw a proliferation of work in the development and use of performance assessments in K–12 education, including the large-scale use of performance tasks. However, much of that work was derailed by 2001 as the era of high-stakes testing and accountability was ushered in by No Child Left Behind.[3] The innovation had been interrupted again.

A little more than a decade later, the interest in moving toward using authentic, performance-based assessments for teaching, learning, and accountability resurged.[4] The skeptic would ask, "So, what's different this time?" We see three causes for hope, which lead us to conclude that the time is right to fully embrace the assessment of authentic performance tasks as an accepted, regular, useful, and meaningful feature of the educational landscape.

First, the construct of deeper learning (and its close cousins, twenty-first-century skills and career and college readiness) has widespread roots among educators, policy makers, and business leaders alike, not only in the United States but around the world.[5] Second, research and development in the field of classroom assessment has strengthened and focused during the past two decades as an appreciation for teachers' use of assessment *for* learning has increasingly been recognized as central to student learning.[6] And third, the principle of balanced assessment, both at the classroom level and at the state accountability level, is increasingly understood and accepted as a basic premise of good pedagogy and good policy.[7]

The conditions, then, for school districts to move toward the integration of performance assessments in their curricula and schools are favorable, but good conditions alone will not bring about a more permanent shift in the assessment landscape. After all, an innovation is not merely something that is new; an innovation is a new way of doing something with the intent that it be a *better* and *lasting* way of accomplishing important aims.

By this definition, laundry machines, personal computers, and cells phones are innovations. They've become accepted, regular, useful, and meaningful elements of modern life. We're convinced that it's simply time to make performance assessments part of the way good assessment is done. To that end, we contend that educational leaders at state and district levels need to focus on two essential factors, both of which sit at intersections of policy and people. Specifically, these factors are the articulation of desired learning outcomes and the leveraging of leadership in schools.

Articulate Desired Learning Outcomes for Students

Backward-mapping has long been a design principle of the curriculum development process.[8] One essentially asks, "What do we want students to know, understand, be able to do, and value?" Once we answer that (admittedly, complex) question, then we work backward, articulating a structured sequence of learning experiences and learning targets, which leads to students' acquisition of desired learning outcomes. Therefore, a necessary policy move in promoting deeper learning is to articulate a set of desired learning outcomes at each level of an educational system.

The city-state of Singapore is an instructive example. Singapore, which gained independence from the United Kingdom in 1965, is a small, island-bound country at the southernmost tip of the Malayan peninsula. It has few natural resources and, as an island, virtually no room to expand. It benefits from being located at the strait between the Pacific and Indian oceans, which makes it a natural intersection of international shipping.

As a small, island nation, Singapore considers citizens its most precious natural resource and therefore invests heavily in them through education. In 1997, education reform in Singapore took a significant step forward with the adoption of a national policy referred to as Thinking Schools, Learning Nation (TSLN). As part of this national policy, a profile of characteristics of citizens necessary to the survival and prosperity of the country was envisioned.

Collectively referred to as Singapore's Desired Outcomes of Education, these characteristics serve to provide a common aim for a diverse educational system, to drive policies and practices in schools, and to identify criteria by which the effectiveness and achievement of the educational system can be measured.[9] Singapore's profile of a graduate is composed of four characteristics:

- a confident person,
- a self-directed learner,
- an active contributor, and
- a concerned citizen.[10]

Each of these characteristics has been operationally defined and thus collectively serve as broad intended learning outcomes from which the formal curriculum is derived. For instance, a confident person is one "who has a strong sense of right and wrong, is adaptable and resilient, knows himself, is discerning in judgment, thinks independently and critically, and communicates effectively"; a self-directed learner "takes responsibility for his own learning, who questions, reflects and perseveres in the pursuit of learning"; an active contributor "is able to work effectively in teams, exercises initiative, takes calculated risks, is innovative and strives for excellence"; and a concerned citizen "is rooted to Singapore, has a strong civic consciousness, is informed, and takes an active role in bettering the lives of others around him."[11]

Of course, the context of Singapore is quite different from that of the United States, where education is certainly of national importance but also where it is considered a state responsibility. Therefore, the call to articulate and set policy from desired learning outcomes of education resides at the state level. In this instance, Virginia provides an instructive example.

In 1996 (just one year before the release of Singapore's TSLN), an unpublished dissertation investigated the characteristics and degrees of de facto consensus concerning the intended outcomes of public education in Virginia. The impetus for the study was twofold: a relatively recent wave of strategic planning through which school districts were articulating organizational mission statements that tended to include desired learning outcomes and the absence of such a statement at the state level.[12]

Using content analysis methodology, the study found that about 85 percent of Virginia's 132 school districts articulated a mission statement describing desired learning outcomes. More specifically, twenty-two student outcomes were found among the mission statements. The most common desired learning outcome was citizenship, which was evident in 42 percent of the sample. Other desired learning outcomes of education included preparedness for the future, economic productiveness, lifelong learning, and academic achievement. However, no desired outcome was evident in a majority of districts, suggesting a low degree of de facto consensus concerning the desired outcomes of education in Virginia at the time.

Today, the policy context in Virginia concerning the desired outcomes of education is quite different. In 2016, the Virginia Board of Education articulated a set of broad, long-term intended learning outcomes of public education referred to as the *Profile of a Virginia Graduate*.[13]

Broadly, the Virginia Department of Education has described the profile as the knowledge, skills, and dispositions that students must attain in order to be successful in postsecondary education, the workforce, and life. More specifically, students in Virginia are expected to

Purposeful Innovation 121

- achieve and apply appropriate academic and technical knowledge (content knowledge);
- demonstrate productive workplace skills, qualities, and behaviors (workplace skills);
- build connections and value interactions with others as a responsible and responsive citizen (community engagement and civic responsibility); and
- align knowledge, skills and personal interests with career opportunities (career exploration).[14]

These desired outcomes of education in Virginia are composed of five interrelated elements: critical thinking, creativity, communication, collaboration, and citizenship.

The articulation of a broad set of desired learning outcomes at the state level is an essential step in creating a context for deeper learning. These, in turn, are manifest at the district level. Table 10.1 includes examples of profiles of graduates as articulated by a small, a moderately sized, and a large school district, respectively. Each district, in turn, operationally defines these outcomes, as illustrated by the following:

- Hard-working and Resilient: work with purpose, energy, and a commitment to both short-term tasks and long-terms goals; demonstrate the ability to effectively adapt to change; use setbacks as opportunities to learn and grow; demonstrate reliability, diligence, and the ability to focus.[15]
- Wellness: All Century Learners seek balance in a safe environment by attending to physical, emotional, and intellectual needs. We strive to be

Table 10.1 Examples of district-level desired learning outcomes

Example from a small district	Example from a mid-size district	Example from a large district
• critical thinker and creative problem solver • effective collaborator and communicator • ethically and civically responsible • respectful and personally responsible • knowledgeable • hardworking and resilient	• communication • collaboration • critical thinking • creativity • citizenship • wellness	• knowledgeable • problem solver and value creator • resilient learner • cross-culturally competent • personally and socially responsible • thinker and inquirer • balanced • communicator and collaborator

resilient and self-aware, and to make healthy, conscious choices in the best interest of ourselves and others.[16]
- Thinkers and Inquirers: Gather, analyze, and evaluate information and ideas; raise vital questions; come to well-reasoned conclusions; think open-mindedly; driven by curiosity to seek information and engage in research to increase understanding.[17]

Deeper learning is dependent upon clear learning goals such as these that are articulated at both the state and local levels and aimed at transferable, twenty-first-century competencies. These aims then serve as the sources from which to backward-map the coherent sequences of curricula, the targeted and engaging instruction, and the authentic assessment practices necessary to manifest deeper learning.[18] Deeper learning begins with having the end in mind.

Leverage the Leadership Roles of Teachers and Principals

A succinct definition of assessment can be conveyed in a simple, two-part question: What do we want students to learn, and what evidence would we accept that they have learned it?[19] It follows, then, that if we want students to learn to be hardworking and resilient, or to know and practice habits of good mental and physical health, or to be critical thinkers and curious inquirers, or any other of the desired learning outcomes, then the evidence we should be willing to accept of these complex, deeper learning outcomes cannot be adequately garnered from conventional assessments. We need performance assessments, which is the fundamental thesis of this book.

Performance assessments seem to be intuitively appealing to most teachers, but it is also interesting to note that not all teachers are necessarily well prepared to create and use performance assessments. As we have alluded to a few times in previous chapters, the advent of the high-stakes testing movement in the early 2000s derailed much good and interesting work being done with performance assessments in the 1990s. For many teachers who began teaching in the 1980s and 1990s, this constituted an abrupt gap in their experience with performance assessments as teachers.

Those teachers who began teaching during the first decade and a half of the 2000s have only known high-stakes standardized testing as the driver of assessment and accountability in public schools. Furthermore, not only have teachers who have entered the profession during the past few years experienced high-stakes standardized testing as teachers, but this was their lived experience as K–12 students as well. The point is that for many teachers, the use of performance assessments may be intuitively appealing, but it is not necessarily something that they are well prepared to do.

The lack of many teachers' readiness to create and use performance assessments is compounded by the fact that assessment itself is an area of relative weakness for many teachers. More than thirty years of research has demonstrated a relative lack of emphasis on assessment in teacher preparation and licensure regulations, as well as gaps in the applied professional practice of assessment by teachers in the classroom.[20] Furthermore, this relative weakness in the domain of assessment is evident in countries other than the United States.[21]

Clearly, there is a generalized need to strengthen the capacity of teachers to create and use assessments of all kinds for the purposes of teaching and learning, whether performance-based or conventional. Sometimes referred to as *assessment literacy*, this important domain of professional responsibility includes knowledge and skills such as those listed in textbox 10.1.[22]

An understanding of the complex set of competencies that constitute assessment literacy for teachers is a necessary first step. This conceptualization should then inform the content and experiences of teacher preparation programs, the criteria for professional licensure, and the goals of in-service professional development.[23]

Textbox 10.1
KNOWLEDGE AND SKILLS
ASSOCIATED WITH ASSESSMENT LITERACY

- Articulate and unpack intended learning outcomes.
- Understand and appreciate the purposes of assessment and the various forms that classroom assessment can take (namely, conventional, and performance-based).
- Ensure the alignment of classroom assessment instruments and techniques to the content and cognitive demand of intended learning outcomes.
- Ensure the representative balance of intended learning outcomes on assessments.
- Create and use conventional and performance-based types of assessments and tasks appropriately.
- Ensure that student performance on classroom assessments is not unduly influenced by systematic or random error.
- Use formative assessment techniques and feedback to progress student learning.
- Use student performance on assessments to communicate student learning to others and to make instructional and curricular decisions.

Our point is that the assessment literacy of teachers is foundational to the important work of developing effective performance assessments. However, while assessment literacy is necessary for this work, it is not sufficient. Textbox 10.2 lists five characteristics that teachers need to possess in order to lead innovations in the use of performance assessments in classrooms, schools, and districts. Again, the foundation of assessment literacy is a given.

Next, since deeper learning outcomes include mastery of content and high levels of cognitive demand, teachers themselves must have a depth of subject-area knowledge. For instance, math teachers must have a conceptual understanding of mathematics, not merely a procedural application of it. Likewise, teachers of writing must have experience as writers themselves so that they are able to effectively coach students through the inevitable challenges of the writing process.

Because every subject at every grade level includes objectives that target applied, complex, higher-order skills, performance assessments have a role in every subject at every grade level. Thus, teachers who are leading innovations in the use of performance assessments must also have a robust understanding of and appreciation for the developmental appropriateness of teaching and assessment practices. For example, first-grade teachers must understand that learning how to tell time is a complex, applied, higher-level cognitive task for first graders.

Teachers must also understand how certain subject-specific skills spiral vertically in the curriculum from one grade level to the next. The intentional spiraling of the science curriculum, for instance, introduces young students to the scientific method through inquiry-based experiences that begin in the earliest grade levels and continues through subsequent grade levels. The

---

Textbox 10.2
ESSENTIAL TEACHER CHARACTERISTICS FOR DEVELOPING PERFORMANCE ASSESSMENTS:

- assessment literacy;
- depth of subject-area expertise (both conceptual and as organized in the curriculum);
- understanding of human development (and the vertical sequence of the curriculum);
- advocacy for and skill in the use of engaging, learner-centered instructional methods; and
- capacity for teacher leadership.

intent is the cumulative deepening, expanding, reinforcing, and refining of a student's ability to apply the scientific method in increasingly sophisticated and effective ways.

A fourth characteristic of teachers who are innovating assessment practices in classrooms, schools, and districts is grounded in the inherent relationship between instruction and assessment. As a general pedagogical principle, what we want students to learn (i.e., curriculum) should indeed be what we teach (i.e., through instruction) and for which we also seek evidence of student learning (i.e., assessment).

Effective teachers align curriculum, instruction, and assessment.[24] Therefore, if performance assessments are intended to engage students deeply in content, in ways that tap the highest levels of cognition and that draw upon authentic, meaningful tasks to do so, then teachers' instruction should do the same. This call for genuine, engaging, learner-centered instructional practices is not new.[25] However, when attempting to bring innovative assessment practices to life, more than lip service is needed regarding engaging instruction. Thus, those teachers leading such change should already be advocates and users of such instructional methods.

A fifth characteristic is that those teachers who are innovating their use of assessment should also exhibit traits of teacher leadership. Teacher leadership is the capacity of a teacher to constructively influence the professional practice of other educators. That influence may come about informally or through a more official leadership role, such as grade-level leader or department chair.[26]

Either way, teacher leadership is utterly dependent upon (1) the expert knowledge and skills that a teacher actually demonstrates in practice and (2) a teacher's ability to model, explain, and coach (informally or formally) others toward effective practice.[27] In other words, teacher leaders are not only excellent teachers; they are excellent teachers of teachers.

Of course, schools and districts do have individuals who are charged with formal responsibilities for leading educational programs, and the focus of this book has been on the role of those district-level leaders. However, the role of building-level leadership—namely, principals—is central to enacting a move toward the use of authentic performance assessments in teaching.

A comprehensive study of school leadership determined that school-level leadership is second only to the effective instructional practices of teachers in impacting student learning outcomes. What's more, this body of research suggests that leadership has the greatest impact in areas in which the need is greatest.[28] Given the relative novelty of integrating performance assessments into both instructional and accountability practices after nearly two decades of an almost exclusive focus on conventional, standardized testing systems, the imperative for instructional leadership is great.

> **Textbox 10.3**
> **KEY LEADERSHIP STEPS FOR**
> **PRINCIPAL'S SUPPORT OF THE**
> **INNOVATIVE USE OF PERFORMANCE ASSESSMENT**
>
> - Deeply understand the purposes and principles of good assessment practices in general and good performance assessment practices in particular.
> - Create a culture for innovative practice and risk taking.
> - Facilitate necessary curricular changes to support the use of performance assessments.
> - Supervise the use of engaging, learner-centered instructional methods
> - Guide the formative use of performance assessment results to advance teaching and learning.

How can principals support the initial efforts and sustained use of innovative performance assessments? First (and as listed in textbox 10.3), it is a basic tenet of leadership that you can't lead what you don't know. Therefore, principals (like teachers) need to possess strong assessment literacy. This need not mean that principals must necessarily possess the highest level of expertise in the domain of creating and using assessment practices to progress student learning, but it does mean that principals must be facile enough in the principles (no pun intended) of assessment to guide teachers toward more effective practice and away from erroneous understandings and poor practice.

Second, principals must create a context for innovative practice within their schools. The culture of a school does not rest upon the experiences associated with one event, program, or initiative; rather, a school's culture necessarily evolves, manifests, and continues to change over time. Nonetheless, fostering and supporting a culture of risk taking is important when promoting the innovative development and use of performance assessments. Such leadership practices include, but are not limited to the following:

1. rewarding small steps toward the use of performance assessments;
2. providing teachers time to share ideas about, examples of, and experiences with performance assessments;
3. encouraging teachers to take risks and supporting them (and not undermining them) as they learn from their mistakes;
4. emphasizing that the best assessments are developed over time and with repeated use; and

5. identifying and acquiring resources for teachers' development of assessments.[29]

As a third practice, principals should facilitate the requisite curriculum development work associated with the use of performance assessments. For example, performance assessments tend to require more time than conventional assessments; therefore, teachers may need support, direction, and perhaps simply permission to revise pacing guides to make room for performance tasks in the calendar year.

Principals' leadership of curriculum development should extend to facilitating the discussion and decision making necessary to make interdisciplinary connections horizontally across the curriculum. Similarly, principals should facilitate the work of identifying key performance assessments that may sequence vertically in the curriculum between grade levels, such as the example of repeated (but expanded and deepened) performance tasks involving scientific inquiry.

As a fourth practice, principals must promote the use of engaging instructional methods that lead to deeper learning outcomes. Such work has long been the focus of instructional leadership in school.[30] Thus, principals can support teachers in identifying specific instructional methods, strategies, and techniques that facilitate student engagement and deeper learning, including those alluded to in this chapter and the previous chapter.[31] Also in the vein of instructional leadership, principals may observe for and coach teachers in their effective use of these instructional methods.[32]

Fifth, principals can prompt and facilitate the formative uses of the results of performance assessments. Such work can involve reviewing student work samples to validate learning outcomes and to critique and improve performance assessments for future use. Making use of assessment results can involve evaluating the efficacy of instructional units and instructional approaches, also with an eye toward improving future practices. Of course, the review of student work samples can be used to provide instructive feedback to students, to reteach, and to extend experiences, all aimed at further progressing student learning.[33]

In summary, principals can lead and facilitate the innovative use of performance assessments in their schools by attending to their own knowledge and skills; leveraging a constructive school culture; and facilitating effective practices in curriculum, instruction, and assessment.

Keep the Learner in Mind

Pursuing the innovation of assessment practices involves state, district, and classroom levels, as well as policies, practices, and the people to implement them. But there is one more group to consider—the students. By definition, performance assessments have students think and do. Performance assessments not only engage the brain; they require students to perform a task and, in many cases, to produce something.

For students whose educational experiences have heretofore been dominated by conventional assessment practices, the move to the balanced use of performance assessments may present some issues, such as uncertainty about the more open-ended nature of performance assessments, difficulty managing time while engaging in a prolonged task, or concern about scoring criteria. These concerns are to be expected; therefore, keeping in mind some guiding principles for navigating educational change is important.[34]

For instance, for students (as well as teachers, principals, and even parents), it is important to keep in mind that change is a process and not an event; as such, it is iterative in nature and will take time. There will be high points of enthusiasm and implementation dips. Students and adults alike will need to cognitively understand the change and affectively buy into the innovation, but both of these may not take root fully until they have had actual experiences with completing performance assessments.

On a more positive note, once performance assessments become part of regular and expected practice in a school, the opportunity for learners to harness deeper learning outcomes becomes greater. This is because performance assessments have the potential to serve not only as assessments *of* learning but also as assessments *for* learning. For example, well-designed performance assessments that are unit-embedded or complex projects integrate instructional and learning experiences as part of the performance tasks themselves. These types of performance assessments depend upon teachers monitoring, guiding, and providing feedback as students engage in the tasks, thus blending the acts of learning and assessment.

Performance assessments can also prompt developing important learning outcomes associated with self-reflection and ownership of learning. Well-designed performance assessments require students to think at the higher levels of cognitive demand, to wrestle with complex problems that do not have simple solutions, to persevere through confusion and errors, to come up with ways of applying prior knowledge and skills to novel situations, and sometimes to identify gaps in their knowledge and skills and to figure out how to learn new ideas or techniques to tackle a task.

When performance assessments put these kinds of demands on students, they develop students' capacities to self-evaluate, self-reflect, self-direct, and learn to learn. In such instances, we think of performance assessments not only as assessments *of* and *for* learning, but also as assessments *as* learning, suggesting that the ability to self-assess is an important learning outcome in and of itself.

SUMMARY

In the opening paragraphs of this chapter, we quoted Grant Wiggins from 1989 when he called for a return to a better way of assessing student learning through the use of authentic performance tasks. We conclude with another quotation from him: "Assessment is the Trojan horse of school reform."[35]

Wiggins's observation is a compelling one, and one that we think resides at the core of this book. To that end, this chapter posited these key takeaways:

- The use of performance tasks for purposes of teaching, learning, and assessing is not new; however, the current confluence of positive factors suggests that states, districts, schools, and classroom teachers have an opportunity to move toward their more effective and more widespread use.
- Integral to the innovative use of performance tasks is clarity about the ultimate aims of our educational institutions, as articulated in profiles of the characteristics of graduates and, importantly, clarity about the aim of deeper learning.
- Also integral to this innovation is the wise leadership of policy makers, district leaders, principals, and assistant principals. But equally important is fostering and leveraging the capacity of teacher leaders to create and sustain this innovative practice with the most direct beneficiaries of our educational programs: students.

Simply put, the design, development, and use of performance assessments for purposes of both teaching and accountability is not an end in itself but a means toward the educational aim of preparing students to confront the challenges and seize the opportunities of twenty-first-century college, career, and life. If that is our intent for our students' future, then the time for us as educators to act is now.

NOTES

1. William and Flora Hewlett Foundation, "Deeper Learning Defined," April 23, 2013, https://hewlett.org/wp-content/uploads/2016/08/Deeper_Learning_Defined__April_2013.pdf.
2. Grant Wiggins, "A True Test: Toward More Authentic and Equitable Assessment," *Phi Delta Kappan* 70, no. 9 (May 1989), 712.
3. Lynne M. Bland and Christopher R. Gareis, "Performance Assessments: A Review of Definitions, Quality Characteristics, and Outcomes Associated with Their Use in K–12 Schools," *Teacher Educators' Journal* 11 (Spring 2018).

4. Linda Darling-Hammond and Frank Adamson, *Beyond the Bubble Test: How Performance Assessments Support 21st Century Learning* (San Francisco: Jossey-Bass, 2014).

5. Hart Research Associates, *Fulfilling the American Dream: Liberal Education and the Future of Work* (Washington, DC: Association of American Colleges & Universities, 2018); Thomas L. Friedman and Michael Mandelbaum, *That Used to Be Us: How America Fell Behind in the World It Invented and How We Can Come Back* (New York: Picador, 2011); Laura M. Greenstein, *Assessing 21st Century Skills: A Guide to Evaluating Mastery and Authentic Learning* (Thousand Oaks, CA: Corwin, 2012).

6. Paul Black, Christine Harrison, Clare Lee, Bethan Marshall, and Dylan Wiliam, "Working Inside the Black Box: Assessment for Learning in the Classroom," *Phi Delta Kappan* 86, no. 1 (September 2004); James H. McMillan, ed., *Handbook of Research on Classroom Assessment* (Thousand Oaks, CA: SAGE Publications, 2013).

7. Christopher R. Gareis and Leslie W. Grant, *Teacher-Made Assessments: How to Connect Curriculum, Instruction, and Student Learning*, 2nd ed. (New York: Routledge, 2015); Darling-Hammond and Adamson.

8. Grant Wiggins and Jay McTighe. *Understanding by Design*, 2nd ed. (Alexandria, VA: Association for Supervision and Curriculum Development, 2005); Allan C. Ornstein and Francis P. Hunkins, *Curriculum: Foundations, Principles, and Issues*, 7th ed. (Saddle River, NJ: Pearson, 2017).

9. Singapore Ministry of Education, "Desired Outcomes of Education," last updated April 16, 2015, https://www.moe.gov.sg/education/education-system/desired-outcomes-of-education.

10. Ibid.

11. Ibid.

12. Christopher R. Gareis, "The Characteristics and Degrees of De Facto Consensus concerning the Mission of K–12 Public Education in Virginia" (EdD diss., College of William and Mary, 1996).

13. Virginia Department of Education (VDOE), "Profile of a Virginia Graduate," 2018, http://www.doe.virginia.gov/instruction/graduation/profile-grad/index.shtml.

14. Ibid.

15. Goochland County Public Schools, "Profile of a Graduate," 2018, http://goochlandschools.org/hendron/Profile2.html.

16. Stafford County Public Schools, "C5W—All Centuries All Learners," 2018, https://www.staffordschools.net/Page/16175.

17. Virginia Beach City Public Schools, "Compass to 2020: Charting the Course," 2018, http://www2.vbschools.com/compass/2020/landing.asp.

18. National Research Council (NRC), *Education for Life and Work: Developing Transferable Knowledge and Skills in the 21st Century* (Washington, DC: National Academies Press, 2012).

19. Gareis and Grant.

20. McMillan; Pamela D. Tucker, James H. Stronge, Christopher R. Gareis, and Carol S. Beers, "The Efficacy of Portfolios for Teacher Evaluation and Professional Development: Do They Make a Difference?," *Educational Administration Quarterly*

39, no. 5 (December 2003); Mike Schmoker, *Results Now: How We Can Achieve Unprecedented Improvements in Teaching and Learning* (Alexandria, VA: Association for Supervision and Curriculum Development, 2006); Christopher DeLuca and Aarti Bellara, "The Current State of Assessment Education: Aligning Policy, Standards, and Teacher Education Curriculum," *Journal of Teacher Education* 64, no. 4 (May 2013); Thomas L. Good et al., "How Well Do 1st-Year Teachers Teach: Does Type of Preparation Make a Difference?," *Journal of Teacher Education* 57, no. 4 (September 2006); Peter Wolmut, "On the Matter of Testing Misinformation" (paper presented at the SRA, Inc., Invitational Conference, Phoenix, AZ, 1988); J. Myron Atkin, Paul Black, and Janet Coffey, eds., *Classroom Assessment and the National Science Education Standards* (Washington, DC: National Academies Press).

21. Michael O'Leary, "Towards an Agenda for Professional Development in Assessment," *Journal of In-Service Education* 34, no. 1 (February 2008), 109–14; Robin D. Tierney, "Changing Practices: Influences on Classroom Assessment," *Assessment in Education: Principles, Policy & Practice* 13, no. 3 (January 2007).

22. Gareis and Grant.

23. NRC, 11.

24. Gareis and Grant.

25. Ornstein and Hunkins; Bruce R. Joyce, Emily Calhoun, and Marsha Weil, *Models of Teaching*, 9th ed. (Boston: Pearson, 2015); Robert J. Marzano, Debra J. Pickering, and Jane E. Pollock, *Classroom Instruction That Works: Research-Based Strategies for Increasing Student Achievement* (Alexandria, VA: Association for Supervision and Curriculum Development, 2001); John Hattie, *Visible Learning: A Synthesis of Over 800 Meta-Analyses Relating to Achievement* (New York: Routledge, 2009); John Dewey, *Democracy and Education: An Introduction to the Philosophy of Education* (New York: Macmillan, 1916).

26. Diane Y. Silva, Belinda Gimbert, and James Nolan, "Sliding the Doors: Locking and Unlocking Possibilities for Teacher Leadership," *Teachers College Record* 102, no. 4 (August 2000).

27. Lida J. Uribe-Flórez, Amneh Al-rawashdeh, and Sara Morales, "Perceptions about Teacher Leadership: Do Teacher Leaders and Administrators Share a Common Ground?," *Journal of International Education and Leadership* 4, no. 1 (Spring 2014); James S. Pounder, "Transformational Classroom Leadership: The Fourth Wave of Teacher Leadership?," *Educational Management Administration & Leadership* 34, no. 4 (October 2006).

28. Karen S. Louis, Kenneth Leithwood, Kyla L. Wahlstrom, and Stephen E. Anderson, *Investigating the Links to Improved Student Learning: Final Report of Research Findings* (St. Paul: University of Minnesota, 2010), https://www.wallacefoundation.org/knowledge-center/Documents/Investigating-the-Links-to-Improved-Student-Learning.pdf.

29. Tonya R. Moon and Carolyn M. Callahan, "Classroom Performance Assessment: What Should It Look Like in a Standards-Based Classroom?," *NASSP Bulletin* 85, no. 622 (February 2001).

30. Rose M. Ylimaki, ed., *The New Instructional Leadership: ISLLC Standard Two* (New York: Routledge).

31. Joyce, Calhoun, and Weil; Marzano, Pickering, and Pollock; Hattie.

32. Michael DiPaola and Wayne K. Hoy, *Improving Instruction through Supervision, Evaluation, and Professional Development* (Charlotte, NC: Information Age Publishing, 2013).

33. Gareis and Grant.

34. Michael Fullan, *The New Meaning of Educational Change*, 4th ed. (New York: Teachers College Press, 2007).

35. Jay McTighe, personal communication, February 18, 2017.

Appendix A

Integrated Performance Task (IPT)

Table of Contents

This Booklet Contains:

	page
Introduction: Children's Health	1
IPT Situation: Promoting Student Health at Smith Elementary School	2
IPT Directions	2
Document 1 - Fact Sheet: Children's Playground Injuries	3
Document 2 - News Story: Shaping Up with Fruit and Salad at Lunch	4
Document 3 - Advertisement: Fitness 4 Kids Outdoor Fitness Courses	5
Prompt 1	6
Prompt 2	7
IPT Rubric	9

Introduction: Children's Health

Why should children stay active and eat the right foods? Kids who exercise a lot and eat nutritious food have fewer health problems. People who eat well and exercise safely usually live longer than people who don't. We should learn how to be healthy as children so it will help us now and later in life.

Appendix A

IPT Situation: Promoting Student Health at Smith Elementary School

You are a 4th-grade student at Smith Elementary School. A local business wants to give your school money to help improve health for all of the students.

The money will be used to pay for only one of these projects:

- An outdoor fitness course at the school
- A fruit and salad bar for the lunchroom

Some students want a fitness course and some students want a fruit and salad bar. Your principal, Mr. Beach, says the school cannot have both. Mr. Beach wants you to help him make a choice. You should read and think about the information in this booklet. Then choose the project that will be better for promoting health for all of the students at Smith Elementary School.

Fruit and Salad Bar

Outdoor Fitness Course

IPT Directions

- Follow along while the information in this booklet is read aloud.
- You may circle, highlight, or underline important information and take notes as the booklet is being read.
- While the booklet is being read aloud, mark any words that you don't understand.
- There are two questions, or prompts, that you should answer after you have reviewed and thought about all of the information in this booklet.
- All of your final answers to the prompts must be typed on the computer.
- The rubric on page 10 shows how your answers to the prompts will be scored.

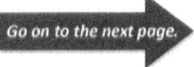

National Council for Playground Safety
ncfps.org

Fact Sheet: Children's Playground Injuries

- Each year, over 200,000 children in the United States are injured while using playground equipment.

- Most of the children are 5 to 9 years old.

- Over two-thirds of all playground injuries take place at schools and other public playgrounds.

- About 8 out of every 10 playground injuries occur because of falls.

- Broken bones make up over one-third of these injuries.

Sources: cdc.gov and cpsc.gov

Go on to the next page.

Shaping Up with Fruit and Salad at Lunch
By Chris Douglas - Staff Writer

SCHOOL NEWS - October 2, 2016

Every day at Midway Elementary School, Diana and her friends get to choose between the regular school lunch and the fruit and salad bar. Most of the time, she picks fresh fruit, vegetables, lettuce, and cheese from the fruit and salad bar for lunch.

"It's tastier," Diana says, "and the fruit is so sweet!"

Diana is one of many students who likes the fruit and salad bar at Midway Elementary School. A survey of students showed that most of them get lunch from the fruit and salad bar.

Local farmers like the fruit and salad bar too. The school started buying food from Midway farmers this year. It costs less to buy local fruits and vegetables than to bring in food grown in other places.

The fruit and salad bar costs less than the regular school lunches. Students pay $2.00 for a regular school lunch. A fruit and salad bar lunch costs $1.50.

A lot of children are growing up on junk food and fast food. But now Midway students can eat healthy foods that they may not get except at school.

The students think the best thing about the fruit and salad bar is having more choices. "I can eat my favorite food or have something different every day," says Diana.

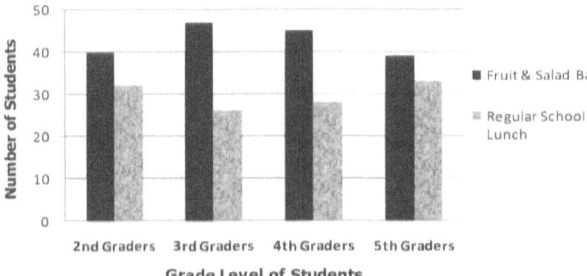

Survey: Lunch Choices of Midway Students

Appendix A

Fitness 4 Kids®

Outdoor Fitness Courses

The only fitness course your school will ever need!

Call today!
1-800-555-3484

UNLIMITED LIFETIME GUARANTEE: Any broken parts on *Fitness 4 Kids* Outdoor Fitness Courses will be fixed or replaced for free. "Just call us and we will be there right away to fix it."

Why choose a *Fitness 4 Kids* Outdoor Fitness Course for your school's playground?

All of your students will be healthier with a *Fitness 4 Kids* Outdoor Fitness Course!

Parents will say your *Fitness 4 Kids* Outdoor Fitness Course is the best thing about your school!

All schools need a Fitness Course from *Fitness 4 Kids*!

Call us at 1-800-555-3484 for more information.

What do our customers say about Fitness 4 Kids Outdoor Fitness Courses?

"My class enjoys our *Fitness 4 Kids* Outdoor Fitness Course every day, all year long!" — Ms. Rosa Mendez, 4th Grade Teacher, California

"Kids use our *Fitness 4 Kids* Outdoor Fitness Course before, during, and after school. They can do it all by themselves!" — Mr. Jeff Mann, 5th Grade Teacher, Florida

---

Healthy 4 Life!

Fitness 4 Kids® helps your students get full-body health. Experts agree that children who eat the right foods and stay active will grow up strong and healthy!

**Call now!
1-800-555-3484**

Appendix A 139

Prompt 1

- Be sure you understand what each prompt is asking you to do before you begin.
- You may use the space under the prompts to write your ideas or a rough draft.
- You do **not** have to write a rough draft.
- **Your final answers must be typed on the computer.**
- Use your best writing, but do not worry about spelling every word correctly.

---

1. Look at the advertisement on page 5 (Document 3).
   - There might be information that is incorrect, unbelievable, or misleading in the advertisement. Misleading means it might lead someone away from the truth.
   - Find all of the information that is incorrect, unbelievable, or misleading in the ad.
   - Explain why you think the information is incorrect, unbelievable, or misleading.
   - Do **not** just list the incorrect, unbelievable, or misleading information. Give reasons why the information is incorrect, unbelievable, or misleading.

Go on to the to the last prompt.

Prompt 2

2. Write a persuasive letter to Mr. Beach explaining your choice for improving health for all students at Smith Elementary School. **You must pick only one of these projects: an outdoor fitness course *or* a fruit and salad bar.** Use information from this booklet to help you write your letter to Mr. Beach. You may also use your ideas from Prompt 1 to help you write your letter.

   <u>You should include all of the following in your letter</u>:
   - ☐ A greeting (Dear Mr. Beach,)
   - ☐ An opening sentence or a topic sentence that tells which project you are recommending to Mr. Beach
   - ☐ Reasons from this booklet that support your choice
   - ☐ A final sentence that summarizes your recommendation
   - ☐ A closing (Yours truly, A Fourth-Grade Student)

   Do not type your name on the letter.

   greeting → Dear Mr. Beach,

   closing → Yours truly,
   A Fourth-Grade Student

The rubric is on the last page.

Appendix A 141

INTEGRATED PERFORMANCE TASK RUBRIC

Critical Thinking (CT): *The student studies the information to decide if it is truthful and important.*

Element	Level 4	Level 3	Level 2	Level 1
CT: Decides if the information in the IPT booklet is correct and believable *(Prompt 1)*	• Gives many examples of information that is incorrect, misleading, or unbelievable. • Gives clear, logical, and detailed reasons why each example is incorrect, misleading, or unbelievable.	• Gives two or more examples of information that is incorrect, misleading, or unbelievable. • Gives clear and logical reasons why each example is incorrect, misleading, or unbelievable.	• Gives one or more examples of incorrect, misleading, or unbelievable information. • Gives reasons why each example is incorrect, misleading, or unbelievable. • Reasons may be unclear.	• Gives no examples of incorrect, misleading, or unbelievable information. **or** • Gives one or more examples but does not explain why the information may be incorrect, misleading, or unbelievable.

Problem Solving (PS): *The student evaluates the information and uses it to support one of the choices.*

Element	Level 4	Level 3	Level 2	Level 1
PS: Makes a choice and gives reasons for the choice *(Prompt 2)*	• Recommends one of the choices and supports it with many well-explained, detailed reasons. • Gives two or more reasons from information in the IPT booklet.	• Recommends one of the choices and supports it with two or more well-explained reasons. • Gives one or more reasons from information in the IPT booklet.	• Recommends one of the choices and gives one or more reasons for choice. • Provides a reason or reasons that may be unclear or not important for making the choice.	• Recommends one of the choices but does not give reasons for the choice. **or** • Does not recommend one of the choices.

Written Communication (WC): *The student uses information and ideas to create a clear, organized response.*

Element	Level 4	Level 3	Level 2	Level 1
WC: Presents information and ideas that are clear, organized, detailed, and written for the intended audience *(Prompt 2)*	• Organizes all information and uses many well-explained reasons that clearly support one choice. • Uses transition words and phrases effectively for the clear organization and flow of ideas. • Always uses complete sentences and ideas with no repeated information, except when summarizing. • Uses a variety of sentence lengths and beginnings. • Uses advanced vocabulary that appropriately addresses the intended audience throughout the response.	• Organizes most information and uses two or more well-explained reasons to support one choice. • Uses transition words or phrases that provide for the flow of ideas. • Uses complete sentences and complete ideas most of the time with little repeated information, except when summarizing. • Uses some variety in sentence lengths and beginnings. • Uses vocabulary that appropriately addresses the intended audience throughout most of the response.	• Organizes some information and uses one or more reasons to support one choice. • Uses transition words or phrases that may not provide for the flow of ideas. • Uses some complete ideas; some information may be repeated. • Uses little variety in sentence lengths and beginnings. • Uses vocabulary that may not appropriately address the intended audience.	• Has information that is unclear or disorganized; there may or may not be support for one choice. • Does not use transition words or phrases. • Uses many incomplete ideas; some information may be repeated. • Does not use variety in sentence lengths and beginnings. • Does not use vocabulary that appropriately addresses the intended audience.

Appendix B

144   *Appendix B*

    Integrated Performance Task:
School Hours for Middleton Public Schools

Situation:

> Middleton Public Schools (MPS) has been looking at a proposal to change the starting and ending times for middle schools and high schools next year. Right now middle school hours are 9:30 a.m. to 4:00 p.m. The current high school hours are 7:30 a.m. to 2:00 p.m.
>
> The proposed plan would switch the schedules so middle school would begin at 7:30 a.m. and end at 2:00 p.m. and high school would start at 9:30 a.m. and end at 4:00 p.m. If the plan is rejected, then the school hours will stay the same.
>
> You work as an assistant to the superintendent of MPS. The superintendent is in charge of every school in Middleton. She wants you to read five documents and make a recommendation to her. You should consider these two issues before you make your recommendation:
> 1. student achievement
> 2. safety for middle and high school students
>
> You **must** recommend one of the two choices to the superintendent. Either accept the proposed plan to switch the hours for middle schools and high schools *or* keep the current school hours.

Directions:

- Read all of the documents in this booklet **before** you answer the prompts.
- You may circle, highlight, or <u>underline</u> important information and take notes in this booklet.
- Raise your hand if you need anything in this booklet pronounced or read for you.
- The glossary on pages 11-12 explains many of the words in this booklet.
- The rubric on page 13 shows how your answers will be scored.
- You do **not** have to write a rough draft. Your final answers **must** be typed on the computer.
- Use your best writing, but do not worry about spelling every word correctly.
- You will have 90 minutes to read the documents and answer both prompts.

This Booklet Contains: page
Document 1 - MPS School Hours Committee Report 2
Document 2 - Research Article: How Much Sleep Do Teens Need? 3
Document 3 - Social Networking Site Page 4
Document 4 - Students' Posts on Twitter 5
Document 5 - Online News Story: Middleton Public Schools Will Switch School Hours 6
Prompt 1 7
Prompt 2 8
Glossary 9
IPT Rubric 11

1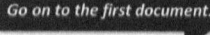

Appendix B

MIDDLETON PUBLIC SCHOOLS

"Middleton schools are at the top of the curve."

REPORT FROM THE MIDDLETON PUBLIC SCHOOLS COMMITTEE ON SCHOOL HOURS

BACKGROUND - Last August, the Middleton Public Schools (MPS) Committee on School Hours was formed. The committee was created because some Middleton parents thought the current middle school and high school hours should be switched for next year. The final decision will be made by the MPS Superintendent. This report explains the options and summarizes the findings of the MPS Committee on School Hours.

OPTIONS - The committee recommended two options:

- <u>Switching the hours for middle schools and high schools</u>. Middle schools would start earlier. High school hours would be later than they are right now. The times for middle schools would be 7:30 a.m. – 2:00 p.m. and high school times would be 9:30 a.m. – 4:00 p.m.

- <u>The other option would be to keep the current school hours</u>. High school hours would still be from 7:30 a.m. to 2:00 p.m. and middle school hours would still be from 9:30 a.m. to 4:00 p.m.

  NOTE - Neither option will affect elementary school hours.

SURVEY FINDINGS - Surveys were given to Middleton students, parents, and teachers to find out which option they liked better. There were mixed results for the survey. About 43 percent of the people who took the survey said they wanted the hours to be switched. Approximately 45 percent said the hours should stay the same. Another 12 percent chose "Don't care."

CONCERNS - Comments on the surveys revealed a number of pros and cons for both options:

- Some parents say they need their teenaged children to leave school at 2:00 p.m. to take care of their younger brothers or sisters.
- Some teenagers report that they have jobs after school to help support their families.
- Some high school teachers say students sleep during classes that begin before 8:00 a.m. If the students fail these classes, they may not graduate on time.
- High school coaches argue there won't be enough time to finish practice/games on unlit fields.
- Coaches also say there won't be enough time for students to shower, eat, do homework, and relax before bedtime on the days they have to travel back to school from away games.

RESEARCH - A previous study from Iowa suggested that high school students should sleep later in the morning. The research is described on the next page, "How Much Sleep Do Teens Need?"

RESEARCH BRIEF
HAMPTON ROADS INSTITUTE FOR JUVENILE RESEARCH

Volume 5, Number 4   February 2016

How Much Sleep Do Teens Need?

A study completed in a large city in Iowa has new information about how later school hours affect high schools. The city changed the start times for high schools from 7:15 to 9:15 a.m.

Health studies show that teenagers have late-to-bed, late-to-rise sleep patterns. Researchers found this cycle is part of the maturing of the endocrine system. The endocrine system affects almost every cell, organ, and function in the body. From puberty until the late teen years, the chemical that causes sleepiness is produced in teens' brains from about 11 p.m. until 8 a.m. This keeps many teens from falling asleep before 11 p.m. Their brains stay in sleep mode until around 8 a.m.

With most high schools starting before 7:30 a.m., students have to get up by 6 a.m. to get ready for school. Up to 20 percent of these students fall asleep when they get to school. Their brains and bodies are still in biological sleep mode. Not enough sleep on school nights can have bad outcomes. Students cannot focus in their first class. They become irritable and have difficulty dealing with parents and peers.

The Iowa research included survey responses from over 7,000 students and 3,000 teachers. About 350 parents were interviewed before and after the start time was changed.

At first parents were worried about how the new school hours would affect transportation, athletics, and child care for younger children. But after the first year, 92 percent of the parents said they liked the later start time better.

High schools reported these facts one year after changing school hours:
- Students said their grades were better.
- Standardized test scores increased in all subjects.
- There were fewer high school dropouts.

Police also noticed safety benefits. Since high school students were not driving to school at 7:00 a.m., there were no early morning traffic accidents that involved teenagers.

The study described in this report is an example of using research in the real world. Now other cities are planning to change the start times for their high schools.

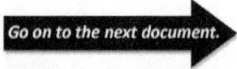

Appendix B

spacebook

Middleton Teens Speak Out 👤 Join

Wall   Info   Discussions

Basic Info

Name: Middleton Teens Speak Out

Category: Organization General

Description: Middleton Public Schools might switch the starting times for middle schools and high schools. We feel that our voices should be heard and that teenagers should be allowed to make these decisions for themselves.

The top 5 reasons for teens choosing our own school hours:

1. School hours affect 10 times more teenagers than adults.
2. If you want us to be responsible citizens, then you have to let us exercise our decision-making skills.
3. My parents pay taxes to support Middleton Public Schools.
4. We are old enough to work so we should be allowed to choose when we work and when we go to school.
5. If students don't like the school hours then they can go to a private school.

The top 10 issues <u>for or against</u> switching school hours:

1. High school kids need more sleep than middle school kids.
2. Middle school students shouldn't have to wait at the bus stop in the morning when it's dark.
3. High school classes count toward graduation and students need to be wide awake for all of their high school classes.
4. More sleep would mean safer teen drivers.
5. Middle school is only 3 years long—high school is 4 years.
6. A lot of high school students have jobs in the afternoon.
7. High school kids need more time to get ready for school.
8. Middle school students need more time to eat breakfast.
9. High school students are grumpier when they're tired.
10. Middle school kids are already used to their parents waking them up for school.

How will the schedule change affect you?

Information

Category:
Organizations – General

Description:
This group was created to allow students to have a voice in their school hours.

This group is seeking to organize students to become involved in their school's policy making decisions.

Open content is public.

Admins

Elaine Coffey (Central High)
Tim Schmoltz (Central High) (creator)

Members
6 of 1,732 members   See All

Events

Events   See All

Final Report from School Hours Committee Presented to Public
May 8 at 6:00 pm

Superintendent Makes Decision for Next Year's School Hours
May 22 at 6:00 pm

Report Group
Share

Create an Ad

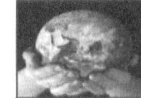

Teen Charities
Kids helping kids. Please donate. Visit teen_charities.com

Teen Jobs
Looking for a job? Thousands of part time, full time, and hourly jobs for teens and high school students
⭐ Top Teen Job Titles
- Host/Hostess
- Server
- Team Member
- Cashier
- Crew Member

Check it out at teenjobs.com

LIFT Energy Bars give you the lift you need!
Visit LIFTebar.com

More Ads

Go on to the next document.

Appendix B

Juan Solo @well_struck · 18m
If they switch school hours, I get to sleep late AND drive to school when there's no traffic — I win!

↩   ⇄   ♥ 7   •••

Ann B @ann_belle · 5m
Juan, it's not all about you. Read Millie's tweet...

Millie Mamoul @millie_mam
Some HS kids will have to quit their afternoon jobs. My mom will need to hire a baby sitter for my sister if I can't get home by 2:30.

↩   ⇄   ♥ 6   •••

Omar Jones @mar_jon · 33m
Who cares if I have to quit my job — I am not planning at working at Burger Mac forever!

↩   ⇄ 1   ♥ 1   •••

Kim D @kimmydean05 · 39m
My dad said don't try to fix it if it's not broke.

↩   ⇄ 1   ♥ 1   •••

Taylor Alvarez @Tayarez · 42m
I always get up early anyway. If they switch school hours, then I won't have to walk home after middle school basketball practice in the dark.

↩   ⇄ 1   ♥ 2   •••

Tony T @cavsrgreat · 1h
My mom won't drive me to school if it starts earlier. I don't want to ride the bus to school!!!

↩   ⇄ 2   ♥ 2   •••

Go on to the first prompt.

Appendix B

DailynewsOnline.com

MARKETPLACE — DEALS SEARCH LOCAL SHOPPING COUPONS
CLASSIFIEDS — JOBS AUTOS HOMES RENTALS LEGALS

NEWS   OPINION   BUSINESS   SPORTS   WEATHER   TRAFFIC

Middleton Public Schools Will Switch School Hours

A source has told us that Middleton Public Schools is planning to change the current starting times of middle schools and high schools. The change will switch the hours so middle school will start much earlier than high school.

This has led to a lot of concern about teenagers driving to school in the early morning hours. In February, a student was badly injured when he was driving to school after 2 feet of snow had fallen the night before.

AP Photo by Thomas Graning
More accidents like this are expected if Middleton school hours are switched.

DailynewsOnline.com asked a few parents about the proposed change. One father said the change won't make it safer. "All teenagers are careless and shouldn't get to drive until they are 20," according to the parent. A mother commented, "How are we going to teach kids to be responsible if they can't get out of bed in the morning?"

DailynewsOnline.com conducted an online survey last week. It shows people don't want the times changed.

Survey question: Should Middleton Public Schools switch the starting times for middle schools and high schools?

Note: Surveys are for adults 18 years of age or older only.	Yes 	29% (14 votes)
	No	69% (34 votes)
	Undecided	2% (1 vote)

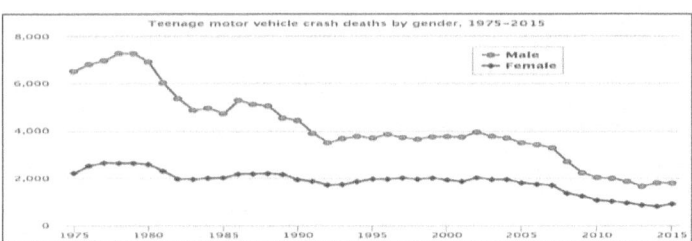

Teenage motor vehicle crash deaths by gender, 1975–2015
Source: Insurance Institute for Highway Safety, Highway Loss Data Institute http://www.iihs.org/iihs

Log in or create a profile to post comments

BAD DRIVERS
Submitted by coolteacher on 02/28 at 7:26 pm.
The graph proves it. Teenage drivers are getting worse.
                1 👍 or 👎 0

IS IT BROKEN?
Submitted by fathertigure on 02/28 at 8:12 pm.
If it isn't broken, why fix it? What's wrong with the way it is now?
                0 👍 or 👎 0

Go on to the prompts.

Prompt 1

> *Make sure you understand what the prompt is asking you to do before you begin writing.*

1. Look at the online news story on page 6 (Document 5 - "Middleton Public Schools Will Switch School Hours").
   - There might be information in Document 5 that is incorrect, misleading, or unbelievable.
   - Find all of the information in Document 5 that you think is incorrect, misleading, or unbelievable.
   - Explain why you think the information is incorrect, misleading, or unbelievable.
   - Do **not** just list the incorrect, misleading, or unbelievable information. **Give reasons** why the information is incorrect, misleading, or unbelievable.

Raise your hand if you need extra paper.

Go on to the next prompt.

Prompt 2

> *Make sure you understand what the prompt is asking you to do before you begin writing.*

2. Write a recommendation to your boss, the superintendent of Middleton Public Schools, about which choice she should make for next year's school hours. You should consider student achievement and safety for middle and high school students.

   Your recommendation should include all of the following:

   ☐ An introductory or topic sentence that clearly states your recommendation to either switch the hours for middle schools and high schools *or* keep the current school hours.

   ☐ A detailed explanation of your recommendation that includes reasons from this booklet.

   ☐ How your recommendation addresses the two issues of student achievement and safety.

   ☐ A concluding statement that summarizes your recommendation.

GLOSSARY

Raise your hand if you need any words or phrases in this booklet pronounced or read for you.

1. **achievement** – (See *student achievement, #64*)
2. **address** (verb) – To discuss, consider, or speak to: *The teacher wanted to address cheating on homework.*
3. **approximately** – About: *She told us we had to wait for approximately 15 minutes; it was more like 20 minutes.*
4. **argue** – To give reasons for or against something: *He always had to argue with his parents about something.*
5. **article** – Something that is written about a topic that appears in a magazine, newspaper, or online: *Did you see the article about Selena Gomez in* People *magazine?*
6. **assistant** – A person whose job is to help another person to do work: *His assistant always took his phone calls.*
7. **background** – Things that help explain why something happens: *We learned about the background of the war.*
8. **biological sleep mode** – A state in which the brain and body are not fully awake: *People who walk or talk in their sleep do not remember anything about it because they are in biological sleep mode.*
9. **benefits** – Good or helpful results or effects: *One of the benefits of working in the lunchroom was free food.*
10. **careless** – Reckless or thoughtless, not safe or careful: *Careless cooks forget to wash their hands before cooking.*
11. **chemical** – An element or compound: *Water is the most common chemical in the human body.*
12. **committee** – A group of people assigned to do something: *The students started a committee to raise money.*
13. **completed** – Something that was finished or done: *She completed her homework in two hours.*
14. **concern** (noun) – An interest, worry, or fear: *Her mother's concern was that she might not finish school.*
15. **concluding** – Coming at the end, final: *The principal had some concluding comments before he told us to leave.*
16. **conduct** (verb) – To do or to perform: *He will conduct research to find out how many kids like school lunches.*
17. **cons** – (See *pros and cons, #50*)
18. **consider** – To think about carefully: *I had to consider both choices before I picked the one that was best for me.*
19. **cycle** – Events or actions that happen again and again in the same order: *The cycle was the same every day—he went to bed late, got up early, and fell asleep while he was eating breakfast.*
20. **current** – Something that is happening now or in the present: *The current president of Russia is Vladimir Putin.*
21. **decision** – A choice that is made about something after thinking about it: *She made the decision to get a hot dog.*
22. **decision-making skills** – How well someone can solve a problem or make a choice: *If your parents gave you $500 for winter clothes and you spent it all on socks, would they think you have good decision-making skills?*
23. **document** – A printed paper that provides information: *Please read the document before you sign it.*
24. **dropout** – A person who stops going to school before graduation: *A dropout has a hard time getting a good job.*
25. **endocrine system** – A group of 8 glands in the body: *A person's growth is controlled by their endocrine system.*
26. **exercise** – To use a right or power that someone has: *Every adult should exercise his or her right to vote.*
27. **findings** – Information or results from a study or research: *The findings showed that smoking causes lung cancer.*
28. **function** – The purpose of something: *The function of the heart is to pump blood to all parts of the body.*
29. **graduation** – Finishing school successfully and getting a diploma or degree: *His family came to his graduation.*
30. **grumpier** – Easily annoyed or angered: *Some people get grumpier when they start getting old.*
31. **high school dropout** – (See *dropout, #24*)
32. **increased** – Higher, larger, or improved: *I am making a lot more money now that my pay has been increased.*
33. **interviewed** – To ask someone questions to get more information: *She was interviewed for the job.*
34. **irritable** – To become angry or annoyed easily: *My sister is always irritable when she wakes up from a nap.*
35. **issue** – A problem or concern that may cause disagreement: *Paying taxes is an issue for many Americans.*

Appendix B

36. **late-to-bed, late-to-rise sleep pattern** – A regular habit of going to sleep late at night and then getting up late in the morning or in the afternoon: *His parents said he was lazy because of his late-to-bed, late-to-rise sleep pattern.*
37. **maturing** – Become fully grown or developed: *She was maturing more every day now that she was in high school.*
38. **misleading** – False, misinforming: *Something that is misleading may cause people to believe what is not true.*
39. **mixed results** – Information that is not clear because some people liked it or agreed, while other people disliked it or disagreed: *The president's speech had mixed results; a lot of voters loved it and a lot of voters hated it.*
40. **motor vehicle** – An automobile such as a car, truck, or van: *You must have a license to drive a motor vehicle.*
41. **option** – A choice or a decision: *My mother gave us the option of staying home or going with her.*
42. **organ** – A part of the body that has a specific purpose: *Your heart is the organ in your body that pumps blood.*
43. **outcomes** – Results, consequences, or effects: *One outcome of studying is making better grades.*
44. **peers** – People who are in the same age group or social group as someone else: *I go to to school with my peers.*
45. **previous** – Happening earlier or before the present time: *She said that she had been a princess in a previous life.*
46. **produced** – Made or created: *We used to have an apple tree that produced delicious fruit.*
47. **prompts** (noun) – Written statements that tell you what to write or say: *The IPT questions are called prompts.*
48. **proposal** – A plan given to a person or a group to think about: *My mother's proposal was for me to go to bed at 9.*
49. **proposed** – Suggested, as in a plan or proposal: *I didn't like my mother's proposed plan for me go to bed at 9.*
50. **pros and cons** – The good and bad parts or ideas about something: *There are pros and cons to going to bed at 9.*
51. **puberty** – The time in a person's life when they start becoming an adult: *The body changes during puberty.*
52. **recommend** – To approve, endorse, or give your support: *I recommend going out to dinner tonight.*
53. **recommendation** – Advice or an opinion: *His doctor's recommendation was for him to stop smoking.*
54. **rejected** – Refused, denied, or vetoed: *The teacher rejected the class's plan to have lunch at McDonald's.*
55. **relax** – To spend time resting or unwinding: *She liked to relax and watch TV when she came home from school.*
56. **responsible** – Mature or reliable: *My mother says she can't wait until I am more responsible.*
57. **research** (noun) – A study or an investigation: *His research was on solids, liquids, and gases.* (See **study, #65**)
58. **rough draft** – A written plan or outline for an answer, a paper, or essay: *Her rough draft included many ideas.*
59. **schedule** (noun) – A timetable or plan of when things will happen: *On my schedule, my last class ends at 4:45.*
60. **sleep mode** – (See **biological sleep mode, #8**)
61. **social networking site** – A website that provides a virtual community of people, such as Facebook.
62. **source** – An informer or person who gives information: *My teacher always knew who did what in our class when he left the room because he had a source.*
63. **standardized test scores** – Results from a test that is given to a lot of students, such as the SOL Tests.
64. **student achievement** – Students doing well in school and learning: *Test scores show student achievement.*
65. **study** (noun) – Research or an investigation: *I just did a study on why some dogs chase cars.* (See **research, #57**)
66. **suggested** – Recommended or advised: *My teacher suggested that I stop sleeping in class.*
67. **summarize** – To sum up, to go over in a few words: *She asked us to summarize the story we just read.*
68. **superintendent** – A person who manages an organization: *The superintendent of schools is the principals' boss.*
69. **support** – To help or to give money to someone: *My father and mother both have jobs that support our family.*
70. **survey findings** – Information that comes from a study that finds out what people think about something: *The survey findings suggested that most people did not agree with the law.*
71. **switch** – To make a change from one thing to another: *I hated the movie so I wanted to switch channels on the TV.*
72. **topic sentence** – A statement that gives the main idea of a paragraph, usually the first sentence in the paragraph: *Her topic sentence explained at the beginning that her paper was all about dogs.*
73. **transportation** – Moving, carrying, or driving something to another place: *Transportation to and from work for many Americans is the bus.*
74. **unbelievable** – Not to be believed, not true, or not real: *It was unbelievable that he ate 36 eggs in 30 minutes.*

INTEGRATED PERFORMANCE TASK RUBRIC

Critical Thinking (CT): *The student studies the information to decide if it is truthful and important.*

Element	Level 4	Level 3	Level 2	Level 1
CT: Decides if the information in the IPT booklet is correct and believable *(Prompt 1)*	• Gives many examples of information that is incorrect, misleading, or unbelievable. • Gives clear, logical, and detailed reasons why each example is incorrect, misleading, or unbelievable.	• Gives two or more examples of information that is incorrect, misleading, or unbelievable. • Gives clear and logical reasons why each example is incorrect, misleading, or unbelievable.	• Gives one or more examples of incorrect, misleading, or unbelievable information. • Gives reasons why each example is incorrect, misleading, or unbelievable. • Reasons may be unclear.	• Gives no examples of incorrect, misleading, or unbelievable information. **or** • Gives one or more examples but does not explain why the information may be incorrect, misleading, or unbelievable.

Problem Solving (PS): *The student evaluates the information and uses it to support one of the choices.*

Element	Level 4	Level 3	Level 2	Level 1
PS: Makes a choice and gives reasons for the choice *(Prompt 2)*	• Recommends one of the choices and supports it with many well-explained, detailed reasons. • Gives two or more reasons from information in the IPT booklet.	• Recommends one of the choices and supports it with two or more well-explained reasons. • Gives one or more reasons from information in the IPT booklet.	• Recommends one of the choices and gives one or more reasons for choice. • Provides a reason or reasons that may be unclear or not important for making the choice.	• Recommends one of the choices but does not give reasons for the choice. **or** • Does not recommend one of the choices.

Written Communication (WC): *The student uses information and ideas to create a clear, organized response.*

Element	Level 4	Level 3	Level 2	Level 1
WC: Presents information and ideas that are clear, organized, detailed, and written for the intended audience *(Prompt 2)*	• Organizes all information and uses many well-explained reasons that clearly support one choice. • Uses transition words and phrases effectively for the clear organization and flow of ideas. • Always uses complete sentences and ideas with no repeated information, except when summarizing. • Uses a variety of sentence lengths and beginnings. • Uses advanced vocabulary that appropriately addresses the intended audience throughout the response.	• Organizes most information and uses two or more well-explained reasons to support one choice. • Uses transition words or phrases that provide for the flow of ideas. • Uses complete sentences and complete ideas most of the time with little repeated information, except when summarizing. • Uses some variety in sentence lengths and beginnings. • Uses vocabulary that appropriately addresses the intended audience throughout most of the response.	• Organizes some information and uses one or more reasons to support one choice. • Uses transition words or phrases that may not provide for the flow of ideas. • Uses some complete ideas; some information may be repeated. • Uses little variety in sentence lengths and beginnings. • Uses vocabulary that may not appropriately address the intended audience.	• Has information that is unclear or disorganized; there may or may not be support for one choice. • Does not use transition words or phrases. • Uses many incomplete ideas; some information may be repeated. • Does not use variety in sentence lengths and beginnings. • Does not use vocabulary that appropriately addresses the intended audience.

About the Authors

Douglas G. Wren, EdD, is an educational consultant with twenty-eight years of experience in public education. After teaching elementary school for fourteen years, Doug served as research specialist and director of research and evaluation with the DeKalb County (Georgia) School District. He currently works as educational measurement and assessment specialist with Virginia Beach City Public Schools and as an assistant adjunct professor at Old Dominion University. Doug holds a bachelor's degree and doctorate from the University of Georgia and a master's degree from Virginia Commonwealth University. His presentations, publications, and workshops focus primarily on assessment development, performance tasks, assessment literacy, and test anxiety. Write to Doug at WrenEdConsult@gmail.com or visit his website: WrenEdConsult.com.

Christopher R. Gareis, EdD, is a professor of educational leadership in the School of Education at the College of William and Mary in Virginia. Originally a high school English teacher and varsity soccer coach, Chris went on to teach English, science, and math at the middle school level, and he also led two middle schools as an assistant principal and principal. At William and Mary, Chris teaches courses in curriculum development, instructional leadership, teacher mentoring, classroom assessment, and program evaluation. He has also served two terms as associate dean for teacher education and is the author of numerous academic and practitioner works, including the book *Teacher-Made Assessments: How to Connect Curriculum, Instruction, and Student Learning*. Chris regularly works with schools, districts, states, and national organizations in the United States and abroad on the design and development of student assessments. Contact Chris at crgare@wm.edu.